LET YOUR VOICE BE HEARD

Endorsements

"In his new book *Let Your Voice Be Heard*, my friend Jack Redmond challenges us to remember and live out our calling to lead people from darkness into the light. I was freshly awakened to the joy of healthy evangelism through the pages of this book."

Dr. Ron Walborn
Dean, Alliance Theological Seminary
Nyack, NY

"Jack Redmond is an important national voice for the church and its impact on culture. He is leading a powerful initiative."

Dr. McKenzie "Mac" Pier
Founder and CEO of The New York City Leadership Center

"If you have a passion to see more people connected to Jesus, you must read Jack Redmond's book, *Let Your Voice Be Heard*. You will be convicted to make Christ known."

Pastor Dimas Salaberrios
Infinity Church, Bronx, NY
President, Concerts of Prayer, Greater, NY (COPGNY)

"Jack Redmond's *Let Your Voice Be Heard* is a straightforward, practical teaching and training on leading lives to Jesus. This book is a must-have resource for pastors to help grow their church by equipping their congregation to help their families, friends, and coworkers connect to Jesus and to the local church. Highly recommended!"

Dr. Robert Stearns
Executive Director
Eagles' Wings

"Jack Redmond hits the nail on the head! We must stop being an echo from the distant past and become an intentional, current-day evangelistic voice! This book is a current-day clarion call for His church to reform!"

Pastor Edward Ramirez, MSOL
Senior Pastor
Harvest Outreach Ministry International, Inc., Paterson, NJ
Dean of Students, Valor Christian College, Columbus, OH

"When you are around Jack Redmond you can't help but be energized and invigorated by his passion for leading people to Christ. *Let Your Voice Be Heard* is the overflow of his heart and will motivate you to fulfill the Great Commission."

Rev. Dr. Adam Durso
Faith Breathes, LLC

"The motto for our local church outreach is 'be a voice to the voiceless.' This book conveys this same message and breaks it down in a simple yet profound way. From the very beginning, the story line captured my attention with the riveting account of the rescue mission at the beach. It progressively causes the reader to examine their walk but doesn't leave you there because it gives practical, biblical answers and solutions. I believe this book will serve as a reminder to the Body of Christ in general, that everyone is vital and commissioned to bring the message of reconciliation, salvation, and hope to a lost and hopeless generation no matter their social status. It also serves as a teaching and empowering tool to those searching for genuine growth and purpose."

Pastor Tania Fuentes
Senior Pastor
Love of Jesus Family Church of West New York, NJ

"Pastor Jack Redmond is a leader amongst leaders with a servant's heart and a desire to see all experience the love that can only be found through a relationship with Jesus Christ our Savior. *Let Your Voice Be Heard* is inspirational and directs us back to the quintessential meaning of being a Christian, to win souls."

Pastor Devon M. Daniel
Senior Pastor
5th Ave. Church of God, NYC

"Jack Redmond has a Word in season! I recommend that every Christian read this book. It is easy prose with great examples, strong theology, and a passionate call for all Christians to awaken our witness, raise our voices, and share Christ's love to a world that is in desperate need of Christ's saving grace. A Christian society has often painted the picture of 'the evangelist' as being the guest preacher at the church last Sunday or the street-preacher downtown warning the backslidden Christians to come back to the Lord. Other Christians would pray for the evangelist and invite people to hear him or her preach the next time they are in town. This picture painted that only certain people were qualified to do powerful evangelism—preachers! Redmond reminds us that in a culture that should no longer be classified as Christian, born-again Christians must no longer silently stand by. This book locates evangelism as part of what it means to be a Christian."

Dr. Antipas L. Harris, D.Min.
Associate Professor, Practical Theology & Ministry
Associate Director, Doctor of Ministry Program
Director, Youth & Urban Renewal Center
Regent University School of Divinity

LET YOUR VOICE BE HEARD

Transforming from Church Goer to Active Soul Winner

Jack Redmond

NEW YORK

LET YOUR VOICE BE HEARD
Transforming from Church Goer to Active Soul Winner

Published in New York, New York, by Morgan James Publishing. Morgan James and The Entrepreneurial Publisher are trademarks of Morgan James, LLC.
www.MorganJamesPublishing.com

9781630476960 paperback
9781630476977 eBook

Library of Congress Control Number: 2015911556

Cover Design by:
Chris Treccani
www.3dogcreative.net

Interior Design by:
Brittany Bondar

This book is dedicated to the men and women who share the love and hope of Christ outside of any spotlight. They are missionaries who live and serve in situations that most would run away from. They are average people in our churches and communities with no name or title besides "Child of God."

I thank God for all of the pastors and ministers, but I believe the Great Commission will be fulfilled through people we'll never know publicly, except on the other side of eternity. I write this book in honor of you.

Contents

Foreword 1

Introduction 3

PART ONE: CREATED TO WIN SOULS

Chapter 1 From the Lifeguard Stand 7

Chapter 2 No Special Title Needed 13

Chapter 3 A Desire for Change 19

Chapter 4 Giving God Away 27

Chapter 5 Loving Others Well 33

Chapter 6 Wired to Win Souls 43

Chapter 7 Finding True Joy 47

PART TWO: WALKING IN VISION AND POWER

Chapter 8 Can You See It? 57

Chapter 9 Restoring the Passion 63

Chapter 10 Go with the Power 69

Chapter 11 Drawn Like a Magnet 75

Chapter 12 Sharing Supernaturally 81

PART THREE: SHARING YOUR LIFE

Chapter 13 Give Somebody a Reason 89

Chapter 14 The Importance of Relationships 97

Chapter 15 Overcoming Our Feelings 105

Chapter 16 Speaking Words of Life 113
Chapter 17 Defeating the Enemy Called Fear 119
Chapter 18 Winning Souls, Not Arguments 127

Part Four: Fulfilling the Great Commission

Chapter 19 Not Pulpit-Driven Only 137
Chapter 20 A Weedlike Faith 145
Chapter 21 Long-Term Passion and Suffering 153
Chapter 22 In Our Lifetime 159
Notes 165

Foreword

There are some books that simply engage the head. The author appeals solely to our intellect with facts and figures. Then there are other works that get to the heart. The pages of the book are dog-eared and tearstained. There is a third category, which is where *Let Your Voice Be Heard* fits into. Jack Redmond has found a way to involve both your head and your heart. You'll be sobered by the task of soul-winning but buoyed by the simple approach he offers. This dual approach to writing will cause you to experience deep change—the kind that is irreversible and destiny-shaping.

I met Jack almost eighteen years ago. He used to walk his dog right past Christ Church—the church where I'm the lead pastor. One evening the music drew him in. This happened a few more times before he decided to accept the Savior as *his Savior.* Jack started attending regularly. I soon learned that this bright, articulate, and inquisitive young man was going to become a spiritual giant. After a few years I asked him to be our youth pastor. Under his leadership the youth ministry grew to over 800 kids. Jack had an incredible ability to connect with outsiders—people on the other side of the Cross who had not yet met Jesus.

Jack's faith was infectious. Tons of kids were converted. It was crystal clear: he had an incredibly big heart for lost people. Though educated in the prestigious Ivy League halls of Columbia University, Jack's demeanor is so down-to-earth that people of all stripes and shapes are comfortable around him. His relaxed style coupled with a passion for souls makes him an excellent teacher on soul-winning. In fact, he now serves alongside of me on the pastoral team of Christ Church—a multisite congregation of 8,000 plus people hailing from over sixty nations. His pastoral assignment focuses strictly on church mobilization. That's just another way of saying: he's tasked with unleashing the congregation out of the four walls of the church and into the world to do ministry.

As I read *Let Your Voice be Heard*, I couldn't helping feeling the same charge William Carey, the old missionary to China, gave us: *"Expect great things from God; attempt great things for God."* Reading this book will equip you to expect a great number of people to meet Jesus through your personal witness. And, Jack's stories and anecdotes will give you the needed boldness to attempt great things for God.

David D. Ireland, PhD
Senior Pastor and author of *The Weapon of Prayer*
www.DavidIreland.org

Introduction

This morning, between five and six billion people woke up dis-connected from Jesus. They come from all walks of life. Some rich, some poor, some with educations, some without, and most somewhere in the middle. They speak every language and have different shades of skin, but possess one thing in common: they have not personally met Jesus. Unless someone shares God's love and redemption through Christ—and they choose to follow Him—they will spend all eternity disconnected from God.

Over forty years ago, Dr. D. James Kennedy in his book *Evangelism Explosion* stated 95 percent of Christians have never led anyone to Christ.[1] In 1970, the world population topped 3.713 billion. In 2014 it almost doubled, to over seven billion. In 1970, Christianity formed 33.2 percent of the religious population worldwide, and is predicted to be roughly the same in 2020.[2]

No significant percentage change occurred, even though we've exponentially increased our ability to share the Gospel through churches, travel, and technology. So even though I support sharing the Gospel through these means, I still believe the most valuable way to share Christ is face-to-face in everyday conversations.

Even though you alone can't talk to everyone, you can reach someone. God does the ultimate saving work, but He chooses to use people like you and me. God wants everyone to know Him (2 Pet. 3:9; 1 Tim. 2:4), and He's already commissioned His followers to spread the Gospel (Matt. 28:16-20). Knowing this, will you let your voice be heard?

PART ONE

Created to Win Souls

CHAPTER 01

From the Lifeguard Stand

It felt like just another summer day at the beach. The sun shone brightly. A gentle breeze blew and all seemed well. The weather felt like a touch of paradise, but this misled many that day. The effects of a huge storm that closed the beaches for several days still lingered. Pretty waves rolled in, but dangerous currents and riptides lurked beneath this beautiful picture.

Our lifeguard staff knew the dangers and though many came to enjoy the weather, beaches were closed to swimming. I relaxed on the lifeguard stand and enjoyed the sun while enforcing the no-swim rule. Children played by the water's edge, but were kept from going into the ocean. Everything seemed under control.

Or so I thought.

I vividly remember what happened next. Someone ran up to me and yelled, "Currents are dragging out several children a couple of beaches down!"

Immediately, I searched the water and identified several objects moving away from the shore into deeper and rougher waters. I looked closer, suddenly overcome by dread. Strong currents were towing about ten children farther and farther from the shore. I knew the water was too deep and the currents too strong for the kids to swim back in. Life and death hung in the balance.

Because of the beach closures, no lifeguards worked on the beach where the children had entered the water. I didn't know for sure, but my gut told me these kids actually belonged to the beach where I worked and they'd wandered off. Parents thought their children were playing safely, but I knew differently. The kids weren't drowning yet, but without intervention, they were minutes from death.

Immediately I blew three strong whistle blasts to signal and activate our lifeguard team that someone was drowning. Our team jumped into action. Instinct and training took over to save precious lives.

Saving Ten Floaters at Once

All about eight to ten years old, the children floated into deeper water in different groups. We needed to get to them before they fatigued and drowned. We needed an extreme team effort to help them escape treacherous waters!

Adrenaline kicked in as I grabbed a floating device we called a "torp" and ran hundreds of yards across several beaches before plunging into the water. As head lifeguard, I swam to the farthest pair of children—the ones in greatest danger—while other lifeguards reached two other groups and secured them with floating devices. This left three groups of people safely floating, but with no ability to swim ashore. Our entire team was engaged and no additional help would arrive soon.

So I swam against the current, towing the first group of children with me. After what seemed like forever, we somehow reached the shore. With these children safe, I shifted focus to help pull in the second group of children secured by another lifeguard with the rescue line. Fatigue loomed as a serious factor for everybody, but we still needed to work.

Once the second group got to shore, I attached a rescue line to my belt and swam through the pounding surf to the last group. At this point, I felt too tired to think straight. Approaching the last group of floating youth, I didn't follow standard procedure and unhook the rope from myself and transition it to another lifeguard. Instead, I grabbed onto the main torp and told the other lifeguard to signal our beach team to pull us in without having the lifeguard belt around my chest. I thought I'd finished, but I was wrong, very wrong.

The group on shore struggled to pull us directly through the same currents that dragged the children out to sea. Even more, the lifeguard belt surrounded my waist. The tide rolled away from the beach so strongly, it pulled me under the water as I held onto the children. I couldn't let go or the current would pull the frightened kids back out to deep waters. At first, the water created a tube over my head, but I knew what would come next. I took a deep breath and the tube of air crashed, forcing me under water.

I desperately held on, not knowing when I'd take another breath. I felt caught in a battle between the sea insisting on death and rescuers fighting for life. Somehow I held on, and after what again seemed like forever, I emerged and breathed air. The rescue team continued to pull until we could stand and walk out of the water.

A potential disaster ended happily because of teamwork. This required extreme effort, but it was a small price to pay to save children's lives. Tragedy turned to triumph and death turned to life because trained-and-ready people cared. It was a privilege belonging to that team.

The Spiritual Comparison

Many people's lives compare to that fateful day on the beach. Everything looks great on the outside, but underneath the surface, deadly currents rage. These internal torrents drag them away from solid spiritual ground, toward emptiness and an eternity without God.

We need to rescue them, to pull them toward the Savior.

Sadly, few Christians feel this need.

The statistics look shocking. Only about five to ten percent of Christ's followers help another person begin a relationship with Him. Our churches often resemble the beach when we saved those children. A few trained and vigilant people spring into action, but the majority relax, unprepared to make a difference by saving souls. A small rescue group can manage a beach, due to relatively fewer lives to save. But spiritually, a small group doesn't work. Every day drowning people surround us, pulled toward eternal suffering. Souls need God's saving grace.

Terms like "saving souls" or "winning souls" mean helping people connect with God through Jesus Christ. This connection occurs when people put their faith in Jesus as the Savior who died on the Cross to pay for their sins. When people accept Jesus Christ in their lives by faith, God forgives them by His grace. This is called "salvation."

That day on the beach, a prepared team of people saved lives at the risk of their own. I've often thought about that day and it's motivated me to share the Gospel—the forgiving and saving grace through Jesus—in a greater way. If I trained my body and mind to rescue physical bodies, I could discipline myself and prepare others to save people from an eternity of utter despair. The thought of people I love spending eternity away from God makes me cringe! But every day, I have the opportunity to help people move closer to a personal relationship with Jesus.

People in spiritual danger surround us all. I pray these pages will equip and encourage us to reach them for Christ. Even more important than equipping, I hope God will awaken a hunger and passion in your heart for the souls of people mindlessly drifting away from their Creator and Savior.

As Christ's followers, He asks us to connect people with Him

(Matt. 28:16-20). Reaching them for Him is a matter of life or death, both now and for eternity. Christ wants to equip, empower, and send us. We each can begin by believing for one soul, praying for one person, and leading that one to Him. Let's get off the spectator's bench and into the game. Above the roaring waves, it's time to let our voices be heard!

CHAPTER 02

No Special Title Needed

When I decided to follow Jesus, my life transformed. Before long I believed if God could change my life, He could transform others. Eventually, I followed a simple pattern: I read God's Word, did what it said, and God did what He promised.

When I realized God wanted to give me inner peace (Phil. 4:7; John 14:27), I prayed for that and He gave me peace. When I needed to change a behavior or habit, I prayed and implemented natural changes. God gave me the strength to change. Soon I realized if God reached out to me for a personal relationship, He also reached out to others. He extended His love to everyone.

So with no title, a few months into my new life God used me to help others connect with Him. As I read the Gospels and the book of Acts, one thing became clear. Once people followed Jesus, they told others about Him. In fact, this comprised basic Christianity for hundreds of years. Not many people held religious titles. As followers of Christ, everyday life involved connecting others with Him. This changed as Christianity grew into a more established religion. However, I believe God wants His people to return to their roots, living and sharing the Gospel like the early days when the Church turned the world upside down.

Almost twenty years after accepting Christ, I hold a church-related title and position, but some of my greatest memories stem from God using me before I accepted an official role in a local church. I thank God He used me to impact lives, connecting them with Him. I'm confident God wants to use us all. Right where we are now, even without a title or ministry job.

The Power of No Title

It's a myth that we need a title or position of authority to do great things for God. This myth causes people not to step out boldly for Christ's cause. Power to do things for God emerges from the Holy Spirit, and He resides in all followers of Christ. The Holy Spirit indwells the person who began following Jesus this morning the same way He occupies a senior pastor with a PhD in theology. We honor those in authority, but more importantly, we honor the Holy Spirit within us and pursue the works God wants us to accomplish.

Typically, pastors and ministers get consumed with running the church, and mostly have relationships with other Christians. These leaders may only connect with people who don't know Jesus when they visit the church. In contrast, congregation members can naturally share the Gospel in their everyday activities and responsibilities. Laypeople go to work, school, or the grocery store, interacting with people disconnected from God. Laypeople can share God's love and purpose with people their pastors don't know and in places they don't go. Laypeople enjoy relationships and connections with people unavailable to church leaders. There may be tens of thousands of pastors, but there are millions of Christ followers. It's simple math. Individuals can influence people that church leaders will never meet.

An Ordinary Day, Saving Souls

If saving physical lives integrated into an ordinary day as a lifeguard, what would our world be like if saving souls belonged to a typical day?

What would our world look like if dishonest businessmen committed their lives to Jesus and lived with integrity and high morals? How would marriages function if husbands loved their wives and wives respected their husbands? Could entire countries change if leaders served Jesus and stopped using and oppressing their people? What if friends, neighbors, and relatives were filled with the Lord's joy instead of turning to alcohol, drugs, or promiscuity to dull pain and escape reality?

Once people choose Jesus, they often need support, love, and guidance to grow spiritually. Serving at a church, I know leaders can't fulfill all the needs for personal, practical, and spiritual support. Ministers and pastors can work twelve to fourteen-hour days and still not meet all the congregation's needs. So where can followers of Christ obtain ongoing support?

They can receive support from laypeople. They can receive support from anyone who follows Christ.

When someone chooses to follow Jesus, personal and spiritual change most often need time. For that reason, a relationship with a new believer is important. Initially, we can share our faith and God's love with someone over time. Then when the person chooses to follow Jesus, it takes more time to grow as a disciple. Patterns of behavior usually need to change. The mind must renew (Rom. 12:2). Someone might see the pastor once or twice a week at church, but few people gain personal access to their pastor on a regular basis. In turn, our presence and support can consistently boost and encourage a new Christ follower. This is why everyday people are important. They can walk with someone, encouraging personal and spiritual victories over time.

That warm summer day years ago, lifeguards hit the unexpected. Those children didn't expect to float toward death. We didn't expect to risk our lives to save them. In a similar way, many people unknowingly face spiritual death. We see them every day. We can help them move toward salvation, if we're willing to risk caring and sharing.

Taking Extraordinary Measures

Jesus said, "Peace be with you! As the Father has sent me, I am sending you" (John 20:21). God calls us to be spiritual lifeguards, ushering His peace into people's souls. He can position us in places to help save people from sinful choices. Are we prepared and willing to dive in?

On that warm summer day, bystanders watched from the shore, hoping we would succeed. Many churchgoers mimic those who stood at a distance, hoping the pastor and ministry team will save everyone. Multitudes of Christians just watch. Others might share their faith, but don't build and maintain a relationship with people until they understand the Gospel and embrace Jesus Christ for themselves.

As lifeguards, we took extraordinary measures to save lives. Just like a lifeguard team, Christians possess the ability to spiritually save lives. Accordingly, I want to invite you on a journey. I'll ask you to train, learn, work, and grow. I'll challenge you to search your soul and leave your comfort zone. As a result, you'll spend an exciting lifetime of helping people connect with Jesus. It may not be easy, but it will be worth it, rewarding you with joy and meaning.

Are you willing to take extraordinary measures to win souls? If you can answer yes, let's begin this journey together. The goal is clear: to seek and save the lost by introducing them to Jesus Christ (Luke 19:10). Will you jump off your lifeguard stand and dive in? Are you willing to transform from a churchgoer into an active soul winner? Will you let your voice be heard?

CHAPTER 03

A Desire for Change

In the presidential election of 2008, the word "change" propelled a relatively inexperienced politician into the most powerful position in the world. The vision and promise of change captivated a majority of the United States to elect President Barak Obama. As millions fell in love with the prospect of change and President Obama worked to produce it, we learned the theory of change can prove easier to embrace than to produce.

Life often exposes our limited ability to bring about desired change through our own strength or abilities. But we still want change. Several years later, presidential debates feature a new group of candidates, all promising change.

The desire for societal change often emerges from wanting a better personal life. At the same time, personal change eludes most people. Afternoon talk shows and nighttime infomercials with the latest self-help gurus or products fill television schedules because people want personal change.

A Gnawing at My Soul

As long as I can remember, something deep within me wanted to change the world. It chewed on my soul, trying to get my attention. I instinctively knew something was wrong and I needed to take action about it. I also felt something was wrong in my life and the lives of those around me. I couldn't put my finger on it, but I knew deep in my soul the answer existed out there, somewhere. I felt like this long before I heard the Gospel.

This gnawing led me to many ideas, thoughts, and actions. Maybe I could plant enough trees and recycle enough things to make the world better. Maybe I could help elect good people to run the government. Maybe I could educate people to improve their lives. So I planted trees, recycled, voted, and taught. As a teacher, I watched in amazement how educated people purposely made poor choices. Despite my efforts, the world around me seemed to get worse, not better. Maybe this perception just reflected frustration with my inability to make a significant difference. Still, something was missing, and I struggled with the reality that I couldn't even change myself.

Meeting the Change Maker

As I struggled with my life and criticized others, I searched for fulfillment. This included playing football, finding the perfect girlfriend, getting an education, locating a great job, or attending the next party. None of it fulfilled me or brought true change until my search led me to the foot of the Cross. After championships, scholarships, college degrees, and human relationships left me empty, I met the Change Maker. I began a relationship with Jesus.

Twenty-seven years on the wrong path ended when I surrendered my life to Jesus and began walking with Him daily. He ushered in true change. Love replaced anger, forgiveness replaced bitterness, and order replaced chaos. I finally found the Person who empowered me to make a difference and observe real change in people. I could lead them to Jesus. I felt transformed, and I wanted others to know Jesus. I began sharing Him and how He offered everyone a new life.

This change message powerfully resonates deep within people's souls. It moves far beyond an economic or political climate. God designed us for a purpose, but many people plod forward outside of it. When we don't live with the quality God intends for us, we look for a way to correct our path.

Still, real change requires the crucial elements of strength and time. By ourselves, we can't access the strength to change and the endurance to walk it out. But thankfully, Christ's strength can flow through us. The Bible says, "I can do all things through Christ who strengthens me" (Phil 4:13, NKJV).

One Person at a Time

Individuals make up our world and its organizations. For a society to change, it happens one person at a time. Individual hearts, minds, and lifestyles must change. Confusion, chaos, and evil undermine God's plans. People create messes through bad choices and the broken structures they build and maintain. What drives them often leads the wrong way. They need new motivation from within, guiding them in the right direction.

As a local pastor, I walk with people through the best and worst times of life. Whether young or old, single or married, most people carry a suitcase full of yesterday's pain. This pain originates through misguided personal choices and other people's actions. This plays out in marriages when a couple brings old wounds into their relationship. These good but broken people find it challenging to get along. Yesterday's pain causes them to lash out today. They're still trying to heal from past pain, struggling not to let yesterday's wounds sabotage their current situation.

In these cases, the first step focuses on their relationship with Jesus and receiving healing for themselves—not to focus on a partner's shortcomings. Only Christ's strength can bring true change, both for people who already know Him and those who don't. For those who don't know Jesus, the first step helps them begin a relationship with Him.

If healing doesn't take place and people walk in their own strength, most often their conflict continues. Sin also enters to medicate the pain or release frustration. As a result, children grow up in a distant or hostile atmosphere. Families and societies form and follow the cumulative choices and actions of misguided people. Changing families, friends, and communities depends on one person at a time. Even as part of a group, individuals can leave their misguided plan and follow God's plan.

Jesus Came to Change Lives

Scripture says, "For the Son of Man has come to seek and to save that which was lost" (Luke 19:10 NKJV). In other words, Jesus recognized that one by one, people headed in the wrong direction. He determined to "seek" them. He looked for lost and misguided people. He wanted to save them from their current path of sin, pain, and sorrow. Yet Jesus didn't wait for people to find Him. He modeled how to enter the houses, the marketplaces, the celebrations, and community events, bringing the Father's love to people and serving them in their environment.

Jesus knew wherever He traveled, He could direct seekers to the right path. Everywhere He interacted with people, lives transformed. And Jesus wanted His followers to do the same. In His final instructions to the disciples, He said, "Go therefore go and make disciples of all nations, baptizing them in the name of the Father and of the Son and of the Holy Spirit" (Matt. 28:19, NKJV).

Lives change when people choose to follow Jesus. When I accepted Jesus into my life, for the first time I had peace. I felt God's love and didn't need to chase the next relationship. God replaced my frustration and disdain for people with love and appreciation. My sinful life of drinking, arguing, and fighting turned into healthy habits and relationships. God transformed my desire for sinful things into a longing for love and righteousness.

Just Doing What Jesus Did

As a new believer, I saw no biblical time limit or restrictions on sharing the Gospel. In fact, in the Bible I read directives like "go" and "do" and "seek" and "heal." So I went. I wasn't waiting around for someone to give me permission because the Word already told me to go.

Two decades later, what drives me each day? Watching God work and transform people. God wants His children to continue His work every day. The most important work proclaims Christ and equips people without religious titles or positions to walk in God's authority, outside church walls. To share the Gospel, the only title anyone needs is "Child of God."

Jesus said, "I tell you the truth, *anyone* who believes in me will do the same works I have done" (John 14:12a, NLT, author italics). The word "anyone" fills me with confidence to serve and share God's love with others. I often say, "You don't need to be somebody, you just have to be anyone and God will use you." God wants to transform and release seated churchgoers into powerful forces in their families and communities. It's a biblical mindset.

Like starving people willing to eat out of garbage cans, many hurting people are emotionally and spiritually starving, filling up with the next sin, the next "thing." They chase things that will never make them happy. Most likely, we watch these people's lives unfold in wrong ways. Are we tired of watching? Are we tired of just talking? Are we tired of feeling like a spectator who can't do anything about it? Whether they're dressed in three-piece suits or changing flat tires, they're spiritually lost. They're disconnected from God and paying a debilitating price for it.

It's time for transformation!

We can affect that change. God created us to not only desire authentic change, but also to be a change agent. This is exciting! We've received the amazing benefits of following Christ, but we can share them, too. We just need to let our voices be heard.

CHAPTER 04

Giving God Away

Excitement hung in the air. Teenagers from the community filled church seats, ready for their friends to sing, dance, or act in our production. Our major goal that night: to share the Gospel with teens who needed Jesus. But God surprised us with more than we expected.

The Christian teens ministered to several hundred people, and after that, I shared the Gospel with the audience. When I asked anyone who wanted to begin a relationship with Jesus to step forward, the altar flooded with teens. As I looked over those seventy to eighty young people, I spotted a white-haired couple standing with them. They were the grandparents of a boy ministering at our event.

Later, I learned these grandparents grew up in a church, but due to unfortunate incidents, they turned away from God and

His people. Their adult children had prayed and shared the Gospel with them for years with little effect. The grandparents knew about God but lived disconnected from Him. However, for some reason that night the Gospel made sense to them. Over time, prayers and conversations softened their hearts. Watching their grandson worship and hearing a clear message of God's love, plan, and redemption from sin finally hit home.

After the grandparents accepted Christ, their adult children approached me, laughing and crying. Their six-foot, 220-pound grandson wept with joy. He knew his grandparents would live in heaven for eternity. Without a doubt, his efforts were worth it.

Giving God Away

The Bible says it's better to give than to receive (Acts 20:35), and the grandparents' salvation demonstrates the joy of a family who gave away God's story. I love that to give away the things of God, we don't need material possessions. In my experience, many of the greatest givers own the least. A lack of physical possessions doesn't matter when "giving God" to people. Great possessions and generous financial gifts can never replace sharing the Gospel and serving people. I believe God created us to give, and givers arrive in all shapes and sizes. They also give generously in a variety of ways: time, talents, finances, resources, and more. Yet the greatest generosity gives away God and His redemptive plan.

For me, the scripture that captures and summarizes God's heart more than any other is John 3:16. It states: "For God so loved the world that he gave his one and only Son, that whoever believes in him shall not perish but have eternal life." The response to the presence of love is giving, and the greater the love, the greater the giving. For those who struggle with understanding God, they can begin with God as a giving God. If the Father didn't withhold from giving His only Son, He will not hold back anything from us that we need. God is a giver and because He created us in His image (Gen. 1:26-27), so are we.

This word "image" means "exact likeness." In other words, we are like God the Giver. Because the greatest expression of God's love is that He gave His Son as a ransom for our sins, our greatest giving means sharing Jesus with others, especially those we love.

Solving the Puzzle

I started sharing Jesus with others just because I could! I knew I had the answer and wanted to tell other people. I often felt like I sat with a group of people watching Wheel of Fortune and I'd solved the puzzle. I acted like a guy jumping off the couch and shouting the answer, "It's Jesus! It's Jesus!"

A few months after Jesus changed my life, I sat in a coffee shop and shared God's love and plan with a friend around my age. The young man's story resembled mine. He'd never heard about God's love like this before. He didn't want Jesus for himself, at least not yet, but I felt joyful sharing the story of God's love and mercy in my life. For so long, I'd wanted to help people, and now I had what other people actually needed.

Later, I spoke to an ex-girlfriend about Christ. I apologized for breaking up with her. She was never the problem. Rather, the emptiness inside of me rejected her.

Neither the coffee-shop guy nor my ex-girlfriend absorbed my message right away. It probably felt like too much. But I hoped to plant Gospel seeds in their lives that someone else could water and harvest.

I'm telling these stories for two reasons. First, sharing the Gospel blesses us with "doing the right thing." Second, not everyone will respond to the message immediately. It's our role to share. It's God's job to change hearts over time. On the other hand, some people did respond to me right away. And I felt incredible peace and authority because I shared God's plan.

Spiritual and Physical Realities

When people resist the Gospel, it's because God's love still needs to sink into their souls. Many problems spring from people's past. Proverbs 14:12 says, "There is a way that appears to be right, but in the end it leads to death." With our own thinking, we often choose wrongly. These decisions might seem right at the moment, but eventually reap negative consequences. In turn, negative consequences usually connect to spiritual issues. Good or bad, current conditions result from a lifetime of circumstances, combined with spiritual choices. The ramifications of recurring sin, no vision or wisdom, uncontrollable injustice, and many times ignorance, accumulate over time.

But Christ renews everything! When He removes sin and its effects, great change takes place. The negative decreases or stops altogether. From there, the life-giving power and love of Christ activates a snowball effect of "getting on track" with the purpose, power, and plans of Jesus Christ.

In the Old Testament, God explained this pattern to His people. He said, "This day I call heavens and the earth as witnesses against you that I have set before you life and death, blessings and curses. Now choose life, so that you and your children may live" (Deut. 30:19).

The Lord described two basic paths to travel: one of death and curses and one of life and blessings. The word "curse" means brokenness, lack, and death. "Blessing" means wholeness, abundance, and life. When we help people choose Jesus, they switch paths in life. They trade curses for blessings, death for life, and brokenness for abundance. We're not asking people just to attend church; they gain the ability to follow a totally different path. People choose the road they walk in life. As Robert Frost wrote in his famous poem "The Road Not Taken," "Two roads diverged in a wood, and I—I took the one less traveled by, And that has made all the difference."[3] At some point, all people choose the wrong path leading away from Jesus, but we have the ability to help them take a different path—and it does make all the difference!

People desire change. They wait. They look down the road. Call to them. Let your voice be heard!

CHAPTER 05

Loving Others Well

I attended graduate school for nutrition and exercise physiology, so I know a lot about health. At this stage in my life, I've talked to certain friends about putting on too much weight. Awkward! How do I tell people they need to lose weight? I don't mean losing pounds to look good. I'm concerned about health. Consequently, I've weathered awkward conversations because I care about people and their health.

Amazingly, most people feel glad I approach them. They know they are headed in the wrong direction physically, but lack the knowledge or motivation to change. I've learned if I approach people with love, the conversation moves from a potential confrontation to a time of warm caring. I can share practical ways to improve their lives.

In the same way, if we care about people, we can learn to

overcome potential awkwardness to address spiritual questions and issues. How much more important is someone's eternal destiny than a few extra pounds?

The Power of Mature Love

I believe love is the most powerful driving force for humanity. The emotions of love grip the soul like nothing else. A mature person understands love is not just a feeling, but also an action. Love can drive people to passion and extremes. But love's greatest expression is good deeds. Sacrifice is easy when driven by love. True love endures and focuses on the things that matter most.

I'm convinced the greatest act of love helps people begin a personal relationship with Jesus. Leading them to Him addresses the ultimate problems and causes of personal pain. If people walk the wrong path, it doesn't matter how well things look on the outside, they're probably falling apart on the inside. They might own many things now, but without God, possessions will mean nothing in eternity. Even with eternity left out of the equation, without God nonbelievers will never fulfill their true life purpose.

I wish I could say that I've always cared about people equal to love's highest point, but reality reveals I've failed many times. I've needed to honestly evaluate myself when I've gotten consumed with responsibilities, or my heart had grown dull from ongoing stress and trials. Thankfully, God and people have forgiven repeatedly and blessed me with a fresh start. I can still love others, and especially love them to Christ.

Focused on the Temporary

When dealing with people disconnected from God, some believers argue and fuss for hours, days, or years with people who need Him. They focus on behaviors, thoughts, patterns, and life-styles, but make little progress, if any. Only Christ can transform minds and hearts, and change people from the inside out (Rom. 12:2). If we could change people with our power or persuasive abilities alone, it would already be done. But this is a "God thing" and requires His power. However, we can facilitate His power through our loving words and actions.

Some Christians fear confrontation and don't want to address people's current or eternal conditions. In our culture, it's not politically correct to disapprove of someone's behaviors or lifestyle. Many people want the freedom to talk and act however they want, without "judgment" from "religious people." In this climate, it can be hard to develop confidence to share our faith. Some are afraid they'll be considered overly religious or judgmental. But if we truly love people, we need to reach the point of speaking up.

Other Christians think if God wants something to happen, then He will do it. It will happen without humans. This thinking contradicts God's Word, which calls us His ambassadors who actively make disciples (2 Cor. 5:20; Matt. 28:19). Yes, God can do whatever He wants, whenever He wants, and He constantly draws people to Himself. He's definitely the most crucial one in the process. But simultaneously, He chose us to physically be His hands, feet, and mouth to bring people to Him. I don't understand it all the time, but this is His choice. Perhaps He chooses to partner with us so we grow closer to and become more like Him.

Whatever the reason, He chose us. In response, we can choose to share His love story.

Harshness or Harsh Reality?

Heaven and hell can be difficult topics to talk about, especially face-to-face. Nonetheless, heaven and hell are realities, whether or not we understand or believe in them. The agony of standing by the coffin of someone possibly spending eternity in hell can overwhelm us. I've heard preachers say the Good News is so good because the bad news is so bad! We're tempted to ask, "Why did it end this way? Why didn't God change things?" The difficult answer is we often blame God for things we neglected to do. Funerals often cause me to recommit to sharing Christ with the lost souls still around me.

Scripture repeatedly speaks of heaven and hell as real places, and one of them will be our eternal residence. Heaven is eternity with God while hell is eternity without Him. Many followers of Christ shy away from speaking about heaven and hell because overzealous preachers in the past have scared or manipulated people to repentance. While this approach was misguided and even abusive at times, it does not change the reality of the afterlife.

Interestingly, hell was never created for people. God prepared hell for Satan and his rebellious angels. Jesus said, "Then he will say to those on his left, 'Depart from me, you who are cursed, into the eternal fire prepared for the devil and his angels'" (Matt.

25:41). Although hell wasn't meant for people, many humans will spend eternity forever separated from God because they didn't accept forgiveness for their sins.

Although God actually saves people's souls and fills them with the Holy Spirit, we can pave the road leading them to Jesus. When we neglect to share Christ, it's often because we don't fathom the reality of hell, and we make false assumptions. But unless we point people to Jesus, they're left in their sin, here and in the afterlife.

Assumption: There's Plenty of Time

Part of human nature believes for the best. We assume people will always be around and there's plenty of time to share Christ. This assumption confronted me when I recently conducted a memorial service for a young man who tragically died in his twenties. He'd lived through many hard things, but always pulled through. When I learned about his death, I spent most of the day crying and talking to others. His life slipped into eternity and I'd never see him again in this life.

Even though I cried more that Friday than I had in years, I felt comforted knowing this young man knew Christ and our church group had encouraged him for years. His life didn't end the way we wanted, but we clung to the hope of seeing him again in heaven. The pain would have been much worse if he'd slipped into eternity without Jesus.

Assumption: People Are Basically Good

This assumption carries a lot of weight and affects actions. But being "good people" does not get us into heaven. The Bible says we're all sinners and this disconnects us from God (Rom. 3:23; Isa. 59:2). So it doesn't matter how "perfect" we are or how many good things we do. All sinners need the Savior, Jesus Christ. Relying on good behavior compares to watching people drive down a road with a missing bridge, expecting good driving skills to save them from hurtling off a cliff where the bridge used to stand.

Sharing the Gospel can be most difficult with morally good people. They often can't fathom their need for a savior. We can also feel uncomfortable because in many ways, their lives serve as an example to others. But spiritually, they are like people driving toward that cliff. Someone warned them the bridge washed out, but they still expect to drive over it. We must reach them with love and wisdom before they plummet over life's edge.

Assumption: Everything Will End Well

In life we face many trials. Over time, we can become conditioned to assume things will work out in the end. We cling to hope. At times, this is a healthy outlook because it keeps us working through problems until they get better. But ironically, this thinking can also create great problems related to eternity. Assuming a good ending can lull us into a false sense of security that we don't need to act. This vague sense can keep us from sharing God's plans with others. This belief contradicts what Jesus said: the Father sent Him, and in obedience He sends His followers to continue His work (John 20:21).

Assumption: They Attended Church and That's Enough

I'm a huge believer in bringing people to church. In theory, if they to listen to our pastor, they will give their lives to Jesus. But in reality, things might be quite different. These people might not attend church. Our pastor might not present the Gospel. The unsaved visitors might not care about the Gospel or like our pastor. Our pastor might speak in "Christianese" and drive them away from Jesus. On the other hand, our friends and family have ongoing contact with us. We can speak into their lives when others can't. Let's shift from faulty assumptions. It's time to act!

Church is important, but it is only part of a process. People harbor many questions, concerns, or flat-out objections to Christianity or organized religion as a whole. It may take multiple conversations over time to remove these barriers or fill in certain blanks. A pastor can't create one sermon to address all these issues in one sitting. Our conversations and prayers before a church experience can open ears and hearts. Conversations after church can also fill in some blanks, answer questions, or bring clarity to new thoughts and ideas. Too often, we feel we did our part when we barely scratched the surface.

Chicken Soup from Scratch

If helping people connect with Jesus is new, we can learn as we go. For example, while we were still newlyweds my wife caught a cold. My mother-in-law asked me if I would make her homemade chicken soup. Up to that point, I'd never eaten homemade chicken soup, let alone made it. I quietly laughed to myself and said no to her.

After I hung up the phone, I felt convicted. I knew I needed to make that chicken soup as an act of love. So I called my mother-in-law back asked her how to make it. She ran off a list of ingredients that I wrote down. Then I asked her how much water, spices, onion, garlic, and other ingredients I should use. She replied in her Jamaican accent, "A little bit of this, and a little bit of that."

Feeling inadequate, I stirred my first pot of Jamaican chicken soup. My wife got her soup, with an extra dose of love. Since then, I've learned to make it better than my mother-in-law, and my kids and I often joke about "a little bit of this and a little bit of that." The key to good soup was humility and work.

When we share our faith with people and what God has done, we get better over time. We learn when it needs "a little bit of this" or "a little bit of that." In the same way, we might feel reluctant to talk about Jesus, but can be confident that we won't fail. Any attempt to connect others with Him doesn't fail. Later our words could take root in their hearts and grow.

Loving Others to Jesus

People often give everything they have to those they love. I've been impressed many times at people's tireless devotion to their children, family, and friends. Whether it's day-to-day care for parents or never missing a child's football game, these efforts are admirable, but may not change eternal destinies. Some people drive through the night or across several states to help needy people, but never take along the courage to lead them to Jesus. True love is best demonstrated when focused on the things that matter most.

Loving people well can lead them to Jesus. How can we say we love family and friends if we won't do whatever it takes to lead them to Jesus? In fact, Jesus asked, "Why do you call me, 'Lord, Lord,' and do not do what I say?" (Luke 6:46).

Jesus said the greatest commandment is to love God and then to love our neighbors as ourselves (Matt. 22:37-39). If we follow Christ and walk in His love, it seems unthinkable we wouldn't passionately connect others with Jesus. But multiple churches and individuals have "numbed" to this aspect of loving others well.

If a rattlesnake bit a beloved person, and a family member held a needle and syringe filled with the antidote, I can't imagine they would watch their loved one slowly die without giving them the medicine. It wouldn't matter if bystanders felt scared, someone would inject it. It wouldn't matter if the rescuer had never administered a shot. At some point the urgency would demand action.

What Will It Take to Share?

A huge gap spans the difference between loving people and loving them well. Loving people well demands laying down pride, fear, and inadequacies to help them. Whom do we care enough about that we would do anything for? Whom do we love enough that we can't bear the thought they'll spend eternity away from God and us?

These questions can motivate us to live differently. An anti-drunk driving slogan says, "Friends don't let friends drive drunk." By comparison, I've seen T-shirts that proclaim, "Friends don't let friends go to hell." With 90 to 95 percent of self-declared Christians never winning one person to Jesus, we need to act.

No individual can reach everyone, but don't let what we can't do block what we can do. We love our friends and family too much to include ourselves in that horrible statistic. We can start with who we know. What would family reunions be like if more people knew Jesus? What would nieces, nephews, and the grandchildren act like if their parents knew Jesus? If parents led their young children to the Lord and raised them with biblical principles? We already love these people. Love can drive our actions to connect them with Jesus.

Driven by love, we must let our voices be heard.

CHAPTER 06

Wired to Win Souls

One of my daughters participates in robotics competitions. In a robotics competition, teams of kids begin with Legos, a motor, wheels, and a computer. They build a small robot and program its motor to perform certain tasks, competing against a couple hundred middle-school students, divided into teams. Success depends on building the robot, programming it, and making the parts function properly. Children shout for joy when the robot completes its task; others cry out in disappointment when their creation doesn't do what it's supposed to do.

Judges award points as the robot follows a certain pattern: pressing buttons, picking up items, or pulling down levers. The team designing and programming the best-working robot wins the competition. It's fun to watch the kids cheering on their creations.

I wonder what God thinks as He watches His created children

completing their tasks. I imagine He smiles when they help others connect with Him. I also imagine God's heart fills with sorrow when His children don't share His love and plans with others. It's a crude comparison, but the difference between kids' robots and God's children resides in functionality and timing. God's creation functions, but we decide when to share the Gospel with others. We're not robots controlled by a heavenly computer program, but even better, we are His children led by His Holy Spirit.

Our Spiritual DNA

My wife and I have four daughters. It's amazing how some of their traits model mine or hers. Recently one of our daughters left her shirt on the banister and my wife corrected her. I laughed as I looked at my jacket left on a chair in another room. The same child thinks so much like me, at times I translate what she is trying to communicate to her mom. Down to certain mannerisms, my DNA passed to this child. Another child copies many tendencies like her mom, from likes and dislikes to talents and mannerisms. It's DNA and can't be denied. Genetics wire our children to resemble us.

Each of us inherited genes allowing us to be good at certain things. Some have greater intelligence, attractiveness, athletic ability, or skill in writing, singing, or art. At times, our genetics create success because certain abilities fall naturally to us.

In the spiritual realm, we're wired to be like Jesus. He compelled people toward God, and our spiritual DNA pushes us toward winning souls. In the physical realm, we line up to succeed with our natural abilities. Spiritually, we also line up efforts and energy toward fulfilling purposes rooted in spiritual DNA. But on this spiritual level, our existence and purpose can only be fulfilled when we win souls. Entire churches also reenergize when new people connect with Jesus and lives transform on an ongoing basis.

So many Christians struggle through life unsatisfied because they don't walk in their spiritual purpose. Financial, educational, or career success offers a level of fulfillment, but if we're not winning souls, that success will turn less and less meaningful.

To Seek and to Save

Jesus said, "For the Son of Man came to seek and to save the lost" (Luke 19:10). He came to earth to save people's souls. If we put our faith in Jesus, we're called and enabled to follow in His footsteps. In a scripture verse I partially quoted earlier, He even promised we'd accomplish more than He did. Jesus explained, "I tell you the truth, anyone who believes in me will do the same works I have done, and *even greater works, because I am going to the Father*" (John 14:12, NLT, author italics). The reason we can do even greater things than Jesus, individually and as a church, is because Jesus chose to limit Himself while on earth to being in one body and had a limited time on earth to minister. The Bible records Jesus as doing ministry for only three years. As a church we have many people and many years to continue the works of Jesus.

We can accomplish great works! God can empower and work through us to seek and save the lost. It's all based on what Jesus did on the Cross and through the power of the Holy Spirit, but we are the vessels: the hands, feet, and mouth of Jesus on planet Earth. Throughout the New Testament, Jesus mingled with people by lakes, on hills, and at weddings. He didn't just seek people inside the Temple. He didn't wait for people to approach Him. He lived among the people and brought the Good News to them. Jesus "did life" with people, and modeled the greatest method to reach them with God's love and plans. Each day we can take that same opportunity.

Not long ago I ate dinner with a pastor from India. From humble beginnings, he lives among people who often struggle to survive. During our dinner with a small group, the pastor opened up a bag and gave away scarves, shawls, and books he brought from India. It didn't matter how little the man owned, he purposely blessed everyone. Giving like this flows from the heart.

Like this man, it doesn't matter who we are, what we do, or what we own. We can bless people with the Good News. It's the greatest investment of our time, energy, and gifts we could ever make. We bless people because they're created by God and need Him. The Bible says, "For by him all things were created that are in heaven and on earth, visible and invisible, whether thrones or dominions or principalities or powers. All things were created through him and for him" (Col. 1:16, NKJV).

When my pastor friend handed out piles of gifts, he felt joyful. It's a by-product of giving. We can also feel joyful and blessed when we share Christ. It's a surprising irony. Although evangelism focuses on God's will and blessing others, we receive a blessing, too. We're blessed when we let our voices be heard.

CHAPTER 07

Finding True Joy

This past summer, I watched my children dig a hole in the sand and create a pool of water by the ocean's edge complete with a sand wall. Growing up by the beach, I'd watched this process many times, played out by different children in other locations. Children with smiles on their faces make a pool, build the walls, and then a wave hits. Happiness turns to screeches and disbelief that their fortress could ever be ruined.

Adult life isn't much different. How many times do we believe in a project that washes out? How many of us build temporary relationships on sinking sand? Sometimes life feels like building a beautiful sand castle during low tide. When the tide rolls in, it's swept away as if it never existed.

It amazes me the extent we'll go to in order to obtain pleasure and happiness. Unfortunately, anything the world offers eventually crumbles. Divorces among couples in the movie, sports, and entertainment industries astonish me. We consider these people the best looking, richest folks on the planet. Don't those things make them happy? Why are the most beautiful people often insecure, wrestling with low self-esteem and eating disorders? Why do some of the most successful people secretly feel like failures? Is it because joy can't be bought by humans?

No, it can't.

True joy bubbles up from forgiveness and a personal connection with God.

Before I began my personal relationship with Jesus, I didn't understand real joy. I was an adrenaline junkie, reaching for extremes to achieve things and feel pleasure. But joy constantly eluded me. Over time, the things I pursued became painfully temporary. I needed to learn that happiness depends on what happens, but joy thrives despite the circumstances. True joy originates with the Lord and His peace (Phil. 4:7). It springs from the eternal, from a God who never changes. This doesn't mean we escape sadness or other emotions, but underneath, steadfast strength and joy hold us up.

The Amazing Supernatural

Sad to say, in the physical realm everyone loses in the end. There is a 100 percent death rate. Plus, gravity and age can be terrible foes. Everyone's physical strength eventually proves insufficient. Physical reality is tough. But we can offer God's supernatural intervention. The supernatural that is derived from God exists beyond limitations of the natural world. There is strength, joy, peace, and purpose exceeding anything we can achieve with our own efforts. And the Lord's supernatural power promises new life, void of imperfection, in the afterlife.

Still, while we're on earth, God exchanges our frailties for His strengths. It's a radical act. He trades joy for sorrow, wholeness for brokenness, and purpose for confusion. His Word declares, "For the joy of the LORD is your strength" (Neh. 8:10). Joy and strength extend to those who accept Him as their Savior, and allow the Holy Spirit to direct their lives.

This joy can sustain us during our worst times. We recognize the Lord's joy when speaking to someone going through a terrible trial, but the person functions with a calm and inner strength. Underneath, the person lives in the joy of the Lord. It's unmistakable and available to everyone. Nobody feels absolute joy and calm in every moment, but I've witnessed its presence in tough situations.

This joy isn't cheap. While it's free to us when we seek God's forgiveness, it cost God the Crucifixion, which paid for our sin. When Jesus died on the Cross, He not only paid the punishment but built the bridge to God's Love. Only God's love can remove the fear of punishment for sin (1 John 4:18). This becomes our path to joy. The joy of the Lord is more powerful than the self-improvement plan devised by the latest motivational speaker. Even if the speaker helps someone, a human message only lasts temporarily. The Lord's joy withstands circumstances because it's founded on Jesus Christ, not just a witty person.

Joy on Earth

In the New Testament, people expressed their faith in Jesus in a variety of ways. Consider these responses:

The first thing Andrew did was to find his brother Simon and tell him, "We have found the Messiah" (that is, the Christ) (John 1:41).

Then, leaving her water jar, the woman went back to the town and said to the people, "Come, see a man who told me everything I ever did. Could this be the Messiah?" Many of the Samaritans from that town believed in him because of the woman's testimony, "He told me everything I ever did" (John 4:28-29; 39).

Then Peter said, "Silver or gold I do not have, but what I do have I give you. In the name of Jesus Christ of Nazareth, walk." Taking him by the right hand, he helped him up, and instantly the man's feet and ankles became strong. He jumped to his feet and began to walk. Then he went with them into the temple courts, walking and jumping, and praising God (Acts 3:6-8).

I can't help but hear the joy when I read about these people connecting to Jesus. Each told a different personal story. Andrew was a religious Jewish man. The woman at the well was a Samaritan whom Jews considered a pagan with a sinful history. The crippled man was a beggar who needed physical healing. Though these people represented different, clashing backgrounds, they each found their heart's longing through Jesus.

Even more, they shared their "find" with great joy. Andrew ran to find his brother Peter. The woman at the well could not contain herself and shared with neighbors who probably shunned her in the past. The former cripple shouted and leaped in the Temple courts. Their faces lit with joy over their connection with God.

Like these biblical believers, when people today connect with Jesus, sorrow can turn into joy. We can watch God heal people's emotions, bodies, and minds in surprising ways. God will also restore relationships, improve family dynamics, and change many aspects of people's lives. Overall, Jesus awards them with abundant lives. He told His followers, "I am come that they might have life, and that they might have it more abundantly" (Luke 10:10b, KJV). The abundance begins with choosing to follow Him.

Joy abounds when someone accepts Jesus as Savior. In the person who receives Him; in the believer who shared the Good News; and within heaven's gates.

The Party in Heaven

Heaven's residents take soul-winning seriously. They get so excited, they throw a party when someone accepts the Savior. Jesus explained, "In the same way, I tell you, there is rejoicing in the presence of the angels of God over one sinner who repents" (Lk 15:10). Heaven rejoices when we lead someone to Jesus. It's not about meeting a quota or impressing anyone. Change can be accomplished by just winning one person. We can help angels rejoice as heaven populates with more souls.

Still more, when a person connects with Jesus, heaven also writes that individual's name in the Lamb's Book of Life (Rev. 3:5; 21:27). These names represent people who will live forever with

God. Jesus said, "Do not rejoice that the spirits submit to you, but rejoice that your names are written in heaven" (Luke 10:20).

People Wait for Us

Without a doubt, I believe people wait to hear from each of us. Often when we grasp the need to share the Gospel, "all of a sudden" people in our paths turn hungry for God. We often think we're waiting on God to do something, when actually, God waits for us. Looking back at Andrew, the woman at the well, and the crippled beggar, they waited for someone with the answer; someone to connect them with God.

When my grandmother neared the end of her life, I prayed for two things. First, that she would not die until she gave Jesus her life, and second, that she would not be in pain. She had a huge tumor removed in her seventies and ten years later, cancer once again overtook her body. She decided not to have surgery or chemotherapy again. God answered both of my prayers. Nana asked Jesus to forgive her sins and chose to follow Him. My grandmother also expressed she was not in pain. According to my understanding, she should have suffered with great pain.

I felt both joyful and angry after these answers to my prayers. I was joyful my grandmother repented of sin and now lived with Jesus. I was angry that to my knowledge, no one had shared Jesus with her before I did. How much pain, grief, and confusion could she have avoided? How much joy could she have felt if she'd known Jesus? My grandmother lived eighty-seven years without making a decision for Christ. I'm grateful I'll embrace her in heaven, but saddened she could have spent a lifetime walking with Jesus.

Who in our lives needs the joy of Jesus? Who needs to hear a Gospel voice?

PART TWO

Walking in Vision and Power

CHAPTER 08

Can You See It?

When God called Isaiah to a prophetic role, he saw "the Lord, high and exalted, seated on a throne; and the train of his robe filled the temple" (Isa. 6:1). When the Lord wanted Ezekiel to reach a wayward nation, in a vision the prophet saw the valley of dry bones (Ezek. 37:1). We may not receive magnificent visions like these biblical prophets, but keeping a picture in our mind's eye can powerfully motivate us to reach the lost for Jesus.

Vision is powerful because it grants the ability to see what possibly exists in the future. It allows us to dream, imagine, and wonder what could actually happen. Acting on vision separates the doers from the spectators. Spectators spend their lives waiting and passively watching what others do. This can entertain us, but never fulfill our souls the way active participation does. Embedded in our purpose, we're created to do good works. Paul wrote to believers in Ephesus that "we are God's handiwork, created in

Christ Jesus to do good works, which God prepared in advance for us to do" (Eph. 2:10). We often find purpose and fulfillment in those good works.

There is no greater "good work" than connecting individuals to their Lord, Savior, and Creator. God calls us to specific vocations, but evangelism is the work of all who follow Christ. It's not an option. God calls parents to lead their children to Christ at an early age. We're all called to win family members, friends, neighbors, coworkers, and others to Him. We're to be salt and light to the world, drawing people to the Good News (Matt. 5:13-16).

This is a different viewpoint from that of many Christians. Those who sincerely love and follow Christ don't always "see" or ask God for a vision for evangelism.

A Vision for Souls

A familiar scripture from an ancient book of wisdom warns, "Where there is no vision, the people perish" (Prov. 29:18, KJV). In Old Testament times, no government safety nets or plentiful opportunities existed to help people succeed. A lack of wisdom and planning could literally lead to death. God's people needed vision. Still today, vision targets our efforts. Without vision, there is no clear road map for how to proceed or succeed at anything.

The same principle applies to evangelism. Whether in the church, household, or street, sharing Christ requires vision followed by action. At times, evangelism also needs a plan. No action or plan most likely means nothing gets communicated or received. In another Bible translation, the same warning from

Proverbs claims, "Where there is no revelation, the people cast off restraint (Prov. 29:18, NIV). Another way to look at restraint is how we order our lives. When we receive a vision or revelation to win souls, we will order our lives to purposely help others connect with Jesus.

To hunger for souls, we must allow God to reveal the importance of evangelism to our hearts and minds. We need a revelation from God to uncover and communicate His vision to us.

Some want to invent the next computer; others want to cure diseases. My dream is to see the Great Commission fulfilled in my lifetime. I'm convinced we'll have enough people, travel resources, and expanding technology to bring the Gospel to all people in the next thirty to forty years. It will require lots of prayer, love, and hard work!

No individual, denomination, or group can do it alone. To fulfill the Great Commission, we'll need a vast army of people serving in a multitude of roles. The key is not just a few people doing mighty deeds, but the cumulative effects of small acts multiplied by millions on a daily basis. It's about sharing God's love and plan every day, outside church walls.

The world sends out millions of people backed by billions of dollars every day in an attempt to reach goals, connect with people, and influence them to a point of view. The church should not be outdone by people with less of a mission, no supernatural power, and no eternal perspective.

Dreaming God's Dreams

Are we dreaming God's dreams and envisioning God's visions? What fills our imagination each day? Is it God's will to fulfill the Great Commission? Can we see it in our imaginations? In our daydreams? In our spirits?

The Bible promises, "In the last days . . . I will pour out my Spirit on all people. Your sons and daughters will prophesy, your young men will see visions, your old men will dream dreams" (Acts 2:17). Is there room in our minds to dream and imagine the Great Commission fulfilled? If not, can we make room for it? If we can't see the whole picture, can we envision a small part, our part?

Even if we can't imagine the whole Great Commission, how about imagining one person? Can we envision encouraging and loving someone to Christ? Can we imagine the church as a place where people can begin a relationship with Jesus? We can ask God to help us dream bigger dreams; to see greater life transformations than in the days past. Ask God to show us His heart for the lost. Then get ready.

God Already Sees It

Jesus has already commanded His followers to go and make disciples (Matt. 28:19-20). God already knows how things end. We only know a fragment of the future. But one thing we know is Jesus said to "go" and "make" disciples of every people group (v. 19). God-inspired writers recorded the basics in His Word, and we're guided by the Holy Spirit along the way. God gives us a part He wants to accomplish. We need to recognize that part and move in it.

Growing up on the Jersey Shore, I spent time swimming and body surfing in the waves. I learned to read the waves as they rolled in—how strong they were; when they would break; and the best time to catch them. I learned to judge which waves would carry me the farthest and be the most fun to ride. I couldn't produce a wave or alter it. I could only ride it. But when I learned to "see" the best wave, I rode it to the shore. I enjoyed waves other swimmers ignored. This required a combination of recognition, timing, and skill, but without good waves, none of that mattered.

Spiritually, waves always exist, but we can recognize the powerful ones. We need to recognize the vigorous waves and ride them when God moves in a church or region. There are times of great evangelism, and other times, more focus on discipleship. Either way, the end goal produces stronger followers of Christ and more of them.

From Vision to Lifestyle

Vision structures lives. When people develop dreams for the future, they do whatever it takes to achieve them. They stay up late, wake up early, spend their money, sweat, cry, and fight for that dream. They do this to become rich, famous, or accomplished. What would happen in our world if every Christ follower carried this passion for the Great Commission?

Imagine if every Christian stayed up late, woke up early, spent money, sweat, cried, and fought spiritual warfare for the

Great Commission? People with this type of commitment change the world and shape culture. God looks for individuals and armies of believers who want to change the world for Him. He also will strengthen them. Scripture assures us, "the eyes of the LORD range throughout the earth to strengthen those whose hearts are fully committed to him" (2 Chron. 16:9).

Even with this promise, we often limit God. Because of our insufficiency and inability, we don't believe what He can do. We project our limitations on Him. When we commit to Him and His vision, He strengthens us. Limits leave.

God's eyes roam looking for people to embrace His call to make a difference. His strengthening asks for one prerequisite: that our hearts fully commit to Him. In our strength, we'll fail, but "I can do all things through Christ who strengthens me" (Phil. 4:13, NKJV). "All things" includes soul winning. If we constantly commit our hearts to Him, He will strengthen us to participate in the Great Commission.

Be encouraged! When God gives a vision, He also provides what we need to achieve and live that vision. We often think of provision only in material and monetary terms. But many times, the things we need from God are wisdom, anointing, and favor from Him. Whatever we need, God can bless abundantly, so that "in all things at all times, having all that you need, you will abound in every good work" (2 Cor. 9:8).

With all we need from the Lord, we can let our voices be heard, and see people connected to Jesus.

CHAPTER 09

Restoring the Passion

How passionate are we about winning souls? Does it bother us that every day, countless people die without hearing the Gospel? Does it disturb us that many who hear the Gospel don't understand or harbor intellectual and spiritual roadblocks to receiving it? Does it trouble us that many people within our reach haven't accepted Christ yet? Does any of this upset anybody?

These questions aren't meant to induce guilt, but to gauge our passion for souls.

The questions also paint a picture of a reality many of us don't think about. If up to 95 percent of Christ followers never win one soul to Christ, something isn't right. We must lack personal passion.

Many of us begin our spiritual walk with a passion to share Christ, but eventually busyness and responsibilities consume us and soul-winning zeal wanes. I understand this. While planning a retreat called "The Awakening," the leaders discussed their people's passion for the things of God. The conversation turned to evangelism and we complained the people we lead weren't hungry enough about winning souls. As we continued, I asked myself: *If the people I lead aren't hungry for souls, how am I leading them? If they aren't hungry for souls, how hungry am I for souls?*

Now in my mind, I'm a soul winner. I gave my life to Christ at the first altar call I heard, after a preacher clearly explained the Gospel. I walked away from sin and poured myself into living for God. He used me quickly to lead people to Christ. Over the years, God allowed me to win thousands to Jesus by enabling me to appear on television worldwide, talk on radio programs, write books, and speak at churches and conferences where many came to Christ. As I grew accustomed to people responding to salvation messages and flooding altars, somehow salvation became less meaningful to me. I'd become a professional Christian and even though God incredibly used me, I'd grown arrogant with a cold heart. This was unintentional, but true.

With time, I repented and asked God for a new hunger for souls. The word "repent" means to acknowledge we're going in the wrong direction or we've missed the target. When we repent, we turn around and change direction. I backtracked and refocused on God in greater ways and strengthened my relationship with Christ, asking Him to change my heart once again.

After this turnaround, God restored my passion for souls, but I'm still not satisfied. I must continue to ask Jesus for His love and passion for souls to consume me. I must also lead our congregation to a place where they desire daily to see lost souls come to Christ. In fact, proof of a return to my former passion will be restoring the leaders and members of my congregation to a greater corporate hunger for souls.

As Christ followers, we need to examine our passion for souls. We need to live in God's Word and be led by His Spirit into all truth. The truth includes Jesus coming to "seek and save the lost" (Luke 19:10) and that "anyone who believes in me will do the same works I have done" (John 14:12a, NLT). Put these truths together and anyone with faith in Jesus will seek and help lost people be saved from their sin, by helping them connect with Jesus.

Steps to Restoring Passion

If we've dulled, how do we sharpen our passion for souls? These back-to-the-basics insights can help.

1. Pray. We can ask Jesus to help us view the lost like He does. Love drove Him to willingly accept the Crucifixion. That's passion! Most of us won't face anything close to a crucifixion, but at times we'll encounter spiritual and natural resistance. But honestly, who cares? We will live with Jesus forever in paradise. What does a little social rejection from people who probably don't care about us matter? We can accept temporary emotional discomfort for rescuing someone from an eternity of torment. By connecting with Jesus through a lifestyle of prayer, His heart will become ours.

2. Worship. True worship results in an interaction with God.

Deep worship is communion with our Creator. We become intermingled, consumed, and filled with His Spirit. Moments like this change us, shaping our souls. When God reveals His majesty, this becomes our reality. When the Father's love consumes our hearts, we can't help but feel His passion. We can set apart daily times to worship. I often recommend worship music to help people connect with Jesus. Worship causes movement in the spiritual world. Worship can also help shape our souls to feel like Jesus feels.

3. Read and Study the Bible. I differentiate between Bible reading and study. Bible reading paints the big picture. Bible study digs deeply into a topic.

Many people tell me they don't understand the Bible.

So I ask them, "How much have you read?"

They usually answer, "Bits and pieces, but it doesn't make sense."

At this point, I share my puzzle analogy. The Bible is like a puzzle with each book a piece of a bigger picture. If we leave out books or parts, we can't get a clear picture. To understand the Bible in its entirety, we need to read it through. I once read through the Bible three times in a nine-month period. A little extreme, but the growth and transformation was worth it.

Bible study is different from reading, but it's also necessary. Study focuses on a scripture or topic in a deeper way. We can choose a topic like evangelism and drive it home. We can focus on certain verses and chapters for a clear understanding of a principle to live by. Spending time in God's Word helps us think like Jesus.

4. Memorize Scripture. When we memorize something, it sticks with us and becomes part of our psyche. Whatever we memorize returns and runs through our minds, continually or intermittently, when we don't expect it or when we most need it. When God's Word resides in the forefront of our minds, it can shape the way we think and act. Memorizing scripture can also help us share the Gospel. For instance, John 3:16-17 says, "For God so loved the world that he gave his one and only Son, that whoever believes in him shall not perish but have eternal life. For God did not send his Son into the world to condemn the world, but to save the world through him." I quoted this passage earlier, but it's worth repeating again to make a point.

With words and principles weaved into our minds, we can share them with others without having to refer to resources. John 3:16-17 can help us answer questions and address comments like these:

- How do I know God cares about me?
- Why hasn't God done anything for me?
- How can I go to heaven?
- Religion and God just want to condemn people!
- How can we really change (save) people or our world?

By memorizing just two verses, we hold the tools to answer some of the most powerful questions and arguments that act as roadblocks for people to receive Jesus as Savior and Lord. When we memorize scripture, we can spiritually fight like Jesus fought (Matt. 4:1-11).

Asking God for Souls

Are there things we don't have simply because we don't ask God for them (Jas 4:2)? We know God loves everyone and He wants them to accept Christ as Savior (2 Pet. 3:9). We can pray He will strengthen our spirits, souls, and minds to do His will. Look at what God's Word declares about praying according to His will: "This is the confidence we have in approaching God: that if we ask anything according to his will, he hears us. And if we know that he hears us—whatever we ask—we know that we have what we asked of him" (1 John 5:14-15). As a result, we can simply ask God for a passion for evangelism. We can confidently know He will grant this request.

This passion can guide and strengthen us to become consistent soul winners. Imagine our churches and society if every Christian won just one person to Jesus each year. That's a vision to connect others with Jesus, letting our voices be heard.

CHAPTER 10

Go With the Power

I recently changed my diet and exercise routine and dropped ten to fifteen pounds over a few months. Friends and others asked me what I did because they saw a difference in my energy and weight. They wanted the "secret" and "power" to charge their energy level and drop weight, too. So I shared my secrets about exercise, eating, and supplements. Suddenly, people listened and tried actions they'd never done before.

My friends wanted knowledge-based power for change. They needed information. Sharing the Gospel also requires knowledge to create change. We need to know biblical principles about God's love, His plan, our sin, the possible separation from Him, and Jesus' work on the Cross. Information enables us to discuss faith and grace. But we can't function well with knowledge alone. We also need God-based power. Without the Holy Spirit, it's like owning a powerful car with no gas in the tank. We're not going anywhere. The Holy Spirit empowers and propels us like gas makes a car move.

We need both knowledge and the Spirit so we can function in God's strength, beyond anything we can personally muster.

To Go or Wait?

Jesus commissioned His disciples to spread the Gospel throughout the world. But then the books of Acts records an interaction that, at first glance, seems to contradict the Great Commission.

> On one occasion, while he was eating with them, he gave them this command: "Do not leave Jerusalem, but wait for the gift my Father promised, which you have heard me speak about. For John baptized with water, but in a few days you will be baptized with the Holy Spirit." Then they gathered around him and asked him, "Lord, are you at this time going to restore the kingdom to Israel?" He said to them: "It is not for you to know the times or dates the Father has set by his own authority. But you will receive power when the Holy Spirit comes on you; and you will be my witnesses in Jerusalem, and in all Judea and Samaria, and to the ends of the earth" (Acts 1:4-8).

Jesus commanded His disciples to go. Then He commanded them to wait. Still, this was not a contradiction. He knew they'd face spiritual and natural resistance. They'd need supernatural strength and wisdom. In short, the task would be impossible in their own strength. As an absolute necessity, they desired God's unlimited power instead of their limited human power. It was as if Jesus was saying: "I want you to go, but you can't succeed without the power. Don't leave until you get the power, then go!"

Jesus didn't make a suggestion, He commanded. His followers would enter a spiritual battle and they needed the proper weapon, the Holy Spirit, to win it. In a physical war, an army might enroll stronger, smarter, and more disciplined soldiers than the enemy. But if the enemy uses a better weapon, the inferior army can wipe out the stronger one.

The Spirit as a Weapon

Acts 2 records that Christ's followers waited, and they were "filled with the Holy Spirit" (v. 4). The Holy Spirit is the ultimate weapon in the spiritual war against the kingdom of darkness. The Spirit lives within us (1 Cor. 3:16), guides us into all truth (John 16:13), and gives us the power to successfully share our faith (Acts 1:8). When we walk in obedience to God in the power of the Holy Spirit, we can do mighty exploits on the Lord's behalf. In our own strength and wisdom, we can't walk in that level of victory. By spending quiet time with God, worshiping, and connecting with a local church, we maintain our relationship with Jesus and stay sensitive to the Holy Spirit's leading.

Later, the Apostle Paul instructed early Christians, "Do not get drunk on wine, which leads to debauchery. Instead, be filled with the Spirit" (Eph. 5:18). It's clear we need to receive the Holy Spirit. God speaks through the Holy Spirit so He can lead us.

However, being led by the Spirit differs from obedience to God's Word. There is power in obedience to God's Word because it's His written will. There is also power in the Holy Spirit's dynamic leading, which always agrees with God's Word.

Be encouraged that God wants to empower us to win souls. He calls us to "witness" on His behalf. Witnesses in a court of law report what they saw. Sharing Christ with others begins with describing what we've "seen" Jesus do in our lives. This message, backed by God's power, can penetrate the coldest and hardest hearts.

To the Ends of the Earth

Jesus gave a road map to His followers for where to start and then expand outward. As we study His Word and follow the Spirit, we learn to envision and walk according to God's plan in greater ways. As a simple metaphor, this patterns picking up people for a bus ride. The bus picks up a person or group of people. It travels and picks up more. As it proceeds, eventually the bus fills. God wants His churches and Kingdom to be on the move, reaching out and gathering up new people.

We like to fly on planes and cruise on beautiful ships, traveling to exotic and exciting places. But it's the local bus that carries people to work, the store, or other essential locations. The local bus looks unimpressive but it gets the job done. Like that bus, we need to transport people where they need to go spiritually. Our job gets them to Jesus. We might bring them closer as they journey, or carry them directly to His feet. Like the bus driver picking up and dropping off people, we don't know the details of their journey or final destination, but we're doing our part.

The Power of Who We Are

The Lion King is one of my favorite movies. In this movie, the young lion, Simba, learns a stampede of animals killed his father, Mufasa the king. Simba's evil uncle, who wants to be king, convinces the young lion he caused his own father's death. As a result, Simba runs away. Over time, one of Mufasa's advisors, Rafiki the monkey, finds Simba. In a dramatic scene, a cloud shaped like Mufasa speaks to Simba and says, "You have forgotten who you are." Because Simba forgot his inheritance, his evil uncle runs the kingdom, leading it in a terrible direction. When Simba remembers he's the rightful king, he fights for and changes the kingdom back to its original purpose.

If we're not winning people to Jesus, we've forgotten who we are. We're children of the King with the power and authority to impact anyone. Many people's lives and society as a whole are going in the wrong direction because the right King is not in charge! God uniquely positions us to do what we're uniquely created to do. If we carry the Holy Spirit inside us, we can share Christ with power. We don't need to feel overwhelmed by reaching everyone. We begin where we are. God already pulls on people's hearts. We help the process when we let our voices be heard.

CHAPTER 11

Drawn Like a Magnet

At the end of the Great Commission, Jesus added, "And surely I am with you always, to the very end of the age" (Matt. 28:20b). Jesus is not only with us as we evangelize, He also draws people to Himself like a magnet attracts metal. He explained, "'But I, when I am lifted up from the earth, will draw all men to myself.' He said this to show the kind of death he was going to die" (John 12:32-33).

These facts can comfort and build confidence when we share Christ and His message. No matter where people stand or what they believe, we know Jesus is with us and already tugging at their hearts. When soldiers lifted up Jesus on the Cross, a supernatural process of cosmic proportions began. Jesus started actively drawing all people to Himself. This encourages me. As we help others move toward Jesus, we assist a process He already set in motion—a process only He can complete.

Looking back at the Samaritan woman at the well, she was ready to meet Jesus. During their conversation, she told Him, "I know that Messiah" (called Christ) "is coming. When he comes, he will explain everything to us" (John 4:25). After their interaction, she told friends, "Come, see a man who told me everything I ever did. Could this be the Messiah?" (John 4:29). On some level, she expected the Messiah to arrive, and she believed Jesus was the One.

The Samaritan woman's life also readied her for Jesus. She'd been married five times. That means five broken relationships—or possible deaths of spouses—with the pain and disappointment attached. Now she lived with another man. In her culture, a woman could starve to death without a husband to provide for her. How many of her choices were driven by a need to survive? How much abuse and heartache had she experienced? Maybe she was a nice person living a disconnected and ostracized life. I'm speculating, but it's evident she wanted a new way of living. She wanted the Messiah.

God places a sense of eternity inside every person and reveals Himself (Eccles. 3:11; Rom. 1:20). We can rely on this revelation when we talk to people about connecting with Jesus.

Learning to Trust

When God called Jonah to Nineveh to preach the repentance of sin, the prophet refused because the behaviors of Nineveh's people offended him. He felt the Ninevites didn't deserve God's love and forgiveness, so he rebelled and ran away. Jonah turned a simple calling into a complicated one. He wanted Nineveh punished, but God thought differently. God wanted these people to repent, accept forgiveness, and live out their best purpose. Eventually, after an ordeal with a big fish, Jonah preached in Nineveh and the people turned to God.

We may not understand what God is doing or why, but we can confidently know He leads us to the good. We can trust Him.

Aside from partial understanding, we can also block evangelism by thinking too much. When we start with simple truths, we can move forward with confidence. But when we analyze all the factors involved, we can feel overwhelmed. We may transition from faith-filled activists into immobilized thinkers and philosophers. Or, like Jonah, we may flee. This can happen if we focus on roadblocks and challenges instead of God's love and power. The argument not to do something looms larger than the original reason and passion.

In addition, we can wonder when to share Christ and exactly how to evangelize. When is the right time, right place, and right method? And who are the right people? We're paralyzed into inaction by worrying about "correctness." When we know God's will and simply do it, His power kicks in. How-to details melt away in the heat and power of God's love.

Sharing Without Formulas

No formula for evangelism works with all people, all the time, in all circumstances. Over the years, different groups and churches have used varied methods with success. Through the decades, popular booklets with set presentations have provided a framework to present the Gospel. These led many to Jesus. But society has changed, and the concept of absolute truth doesn't exist in many minds. We can be logically correct, with people agreeing we're right, but they still reject what we present.

Many people don't care what we know and if we're right. They just want to "live a good life" by succeeding and doing what they think seems best. But when people purposely or unconsciously rebel against God, they are fundamentally wrong. In this case, we can share truth in love so they can choose Christ for themselves.

I heard about a wife who wanted her husband to become a Christian so she badgered him to attend church. This created resentment in her husband, toward her and God. When the wife asked her pastor what to do, he asked her, "What does he like to eat?" She looked puzzled and said her husband liked steak. The pastor told her to go home and make him a steak the way he likes it, and not to mention church or God for a while. It wasn't long before the couple's relationship shifted and eventually the husband attended church and committed his life to Christ.

The wife removed her "evangelistic method" and let God work on her husband's heart. When a husband gives his life to Christ and prays for his wife, I advise him to love her as Christ loves the Church (Eph. 5:25). This invites God in so He can change the heart. When hearts open, we can share faith in a powerful way.

Evangelism as a Process

One misconception about evangelism is that an event can

replace what takes time, change, and growth to occur. On one hand, people can make decisions for Christ at church or evangelistic events. On the other hand, people can't make genuine and life-changing decisions without a process beforehand that brings them to that place.

In most cases, people travel a road before they become born again. God's revelation needs to be absorbed and assimilated. It then must be fostered to grow. As God reveals Himself, hearts, minds, and spirits open to spiritual influence and salvation.

God can sovereignly save someone in a moment, but most of the time, coming to wholehearted commitment is a process. Many need their questions answered, doubts settled, and confusion calmed. As God reveals truth to them, the soul-winning process becomes a joy to watch and participate in. God draws people to Himself, making evangelism a process. God does the saving work. We just walk with people on their journey toward Him.

On the evangelism road toward salvation, we help people move one step closer to Jesus as He draws them. We meet them "where they are" and walk through a process with no time limit. The average person won't shift from decades of thinking and training in one conversation. It is possible? Absolutely! Is it the norm? No. Once again, God can move powerfully and use us to win someone to Jesus in a few minutes. But for the most part, it necessitates time and multiple encounters with truth. To come to Christ, seekers must often reject concepts they thought were true. For real change, they must reject their current worldview and adopt a biblical perspective. Many wrestle with this.

Like Jesus and his relationships to people, evangelism is a face-to-face process where we live, work, and play. As Jesus influences people, we can tailor our efforts to their personalities, backgrounds, and situations. As we're led by the Holy Spirit, let's walk in peace, knowing Jesus constantly pulls hearts like a magnet draws metal to itself. We just need to let our voices be heard.

CHAPTER 12

Sharing Supernaturally

Through an angel, God directed the Apostle Philip to head south on a desert road from Jerusalem to Gaza. On his way, he met an Ethiopian eunuch who served as the treasurer for Queen Candace. After visiting Jerusalem to worship, the eunuch sat on the side of the road reading the book of Isaiah, trying to figure out how to connect with God.

The eunuch had just traveled hundreds of miles to seek God. But he faced barriers to worship. As a foreigner and a eunuch, the Jews considered him unclean. He wasn't allowed in the Temple. Despite the eunuch's extreme efforts and unjust battles, he still wanted to understand basic scripture.

"The Spirit told Philip, 'Go to that chariot and stay near it.'

"Then Philip ran up to the chariot and heard the man reading Isaiah the prophet." "'Do you understand what you are reading?'

Philip asked.

"'How can I,'" he said, 'unless someone explains it to me?'" (Acts 8:29-31).

Philip purposely made a connection, explained the scriptures, led the eunuch to Jesus, and baptized him. A life changed because Philip followed God's supernatural leading to impact someone in a natural setting. Church history and legend claim this Ethiopian eunuch returned to his home country and established Christian churches there. All because Philip listened to the supernatural.

The Natural and Supernatural

In our deepest essence, we are spiritual beings temporarily indwelling human bodies. These bodies grow, mature, age, and eventually die. From dust to dust! So in a nutshell, we're spiritual beings living in natural bodies. Through sin, we become spiritually dead or disconnected from God. But when we're born again, we live in the Spirit. Though we functionally live in the natural, God works supernaturally through His indwelling Spirit within us.

In this regard, the Apostle Paul considered our bodies as temples of God. He explained, "Do you not know that your bodies are temples of the Holy Spirit, who is in you, whom you have received from God? You are not your own; you were bought at a price. Therefore honor God with your body" (1 Cor. 6:19-20).

This is the picture of the Holy Spirit (supernatural) living within us (the natural). These verses reveal that as believers God literally owns us, to be used as He sees fit, when He sees fit. This ownership exceeds religious thoughts and attending church. We're on-duty soldiers ready to impact the world for Jesus at any moment. We're ready to serve supernaturally in everyday situations.

When God told Philip to "go south" down the road from Jerusalem to Gaza, it was a vague direction without explanation (v. 26). Did Philip ask questions? Pray and fast? Need multiple confirmations? Philip obeyed and walked the road, without functional details or directions.

After this first step of obedience, God ordered, "Go to that chariot and stay near it" (v. 29). At this point, my mind would ask questions like, "What?" Or, "Why?" "Really, stand by the chariot?" But Philip chose again to obey.

God led Philip into an encounter because He had a plan. Once Philip got close, evangelism happened easily. Philip asked the eunuch a simple question and a conversation began. At that point, God used Philip to win this influential man to Jesus. The eunuch returned home, the churches he planted have influenced Ethiopia and beyond for almost 2,000 years!

Responding to the Supernatural

Every day it's possible for God to use us supernaturally, wherever we are, to change lives. Our obedience might influence an individual, a family, a business, or in Philip's case, a country or region of the world. Often we don't know the results. We're just called to obey, responding to God's direction and supernatural intervention in everyday life.

God used Philip on a road, far away from the Temple. I like the way God orchestrated this situation. He provided Philip with a spiritually hungry man who needed no convincing. This man was searching, and instead of just imparting information, Philip asked, "Do you understand what you are reading?"

"'How can I,' he said, 'unless someone explains it to me?' So he invited Philip to come up and sit with him" (v. 31).

This passage provides a wonderful picture of the supernatural working in a natural setting. God moves on the human heart and this sets up a fresh dynamic. Instead of hitting walls and trying to convince people, we just answer questions and meet needs. Not every evangelistic encounter will be this simple, but some can be. Whether we share the truth in love, sowing seeds for a later day, or God intervenes immediately, we don't need to worry. We just obey and the story unfolds.

Removing Physical Barriers

Most likely, the Ethiopian eunuch wrestled with rejection and unacceptance due to his physical condition. He left the Temple area where he could only listen from the outside and wish to know more. He felt looked down upon and considered inferior and unacceptable.

With God's leading, Philip removed barriers that day. He accepted the Ethiopian, replacing shame and rejection with acceptance and joy. So much so, the eunuch asked, "Look, here is water. What can stand in the way of my being baptized?" (v. 36).

How many people search for God from "the outside," feeling damaged, broken, and insufficient for acceptance by God and His people? How many feel unclean, unworthy, and ashamed to attend church? God wants to supernaturally touch them through us. He wants them to declare, "Yes, Jesus loves me and wants me to know Him. Why shouldn't I start this relationship right now?"

Because we're filled with the Holy Spirit, God's supernatural power, authority, and order also dwell within us. Jesus said, "The kingdom of God does not come with your careful observation, nor will people say, 'Here it is,' or 'There it is,' because the kingdom of God is in your midst" (Luke 17:20-21). By approaching people who don't know Christ, we bring God to them. We might walk past people who feel hesitant or even against going to a church. Because they're unwilling or unable to attend a service where a preacher shares the Gospel, we can naturally and supernaturally bring Christ to them.

Each day we can be used like Philip. We can be supernaturally used by God in natural settings. He orchestrates life-changing encounters, and we just listen and obey. With the Holy Spirit within, we can share the supernatural. We just need to let our voices be heard.

PART THREE

Sharing Your Life

CHAPTER 13

Give Somebody a Reason

The famous reformer Mahatma Gandhi remarked, "I like your Christ, I do not like your Christians. Your Christians are so unlike your Christ." [4]

Gandhi seemed impressed with the person and character of Jesus, as represented in the Gospels. Unfortunately, the actual Christians he met didn't strongly reflect Christ. I don't know if Gandhi concluded this from random interactions, or personal relationships with long-term Christians. Either way, the Christians Gandhi interacted with seemed to drive him from the Lord instead of drawing him closer.

Sadly, many people who reject Jesus actually discard something else. They reject religious traditions, people misrepresenting Christ, critical attitudes and judgments, or some other inconsistent behavior.

Fast-forward from Gandhi to 2010, when I partnered with an evangelistic music festival called Revelation Generation that attracted 30,000 teens. As organizers met the night before to pray, Bob Grom, one of the founders, shared a few words. He knew many teens participating in the weekend might never enter a church to hear about Jesus. Meeting the weekend's volunteers might be the only way they'd feel Christ's love. During our prayer time, Bob said something that stuck with me. He shared, "Give someone a reason to be a Christian."

The Revelation Generation event featured hard rock and heavy metal Christian bands who also played in secular venues. The bands shared the Gospel with a subculture of youth not welcome in many churches. The event offered five stages and types of music, with the primary goal of youth evangelism.

Still, the stages formed only one method of sharing Christ. The other ways were personal. Thousands of teens accepted Jesus because loving Christians talked with them. Hundreds of counselors spent the day starting conversations and sharing God's love and plan of redemption. In addition, interviewers talked to singers and rappers about their personal relationship with Jesus. Teens asked questions and each interview ended with the opportunity to pray and begin a relationship with Jesus. These additional methods allowed for personal and interactive sharing. The teens actually talked with Christians to understand how Jesus affected real life.

The Gospel Produces Fruit

I love when my experience matches the Bible. At times I've

ignored opinions that certain people or groups would not accept the Gospel. When I ignored what naysayers said and shared God's grace and my story, at least some people committed to following Jesus. The Apostle Paul placed no limits on the Gospel. He wrote, "All over the world this Gospel is bearing fruit and growing, just as it has been doing among you since the day you heard it and understood God's grace in all its truth" (Col. 1:6).

"All over the world." The Gospel can go anywhere and it works everywhere! Every country, every people group, all over the world, the Gospel should be producing fruit of souls saved. The Gospel isn't meant for one race, color, or ethnicity. It's for every people group. It paves the way for a relationship with the Creator of humanity. Humanity has created thousands of philosophies, religions, and ways to live. But Colossians 1:3-6 declares there is one "true message" and that's the Gospel of Jesus Christ (v. 5). The Apostle Paul clearly states "this Gospel" grows "throughout the whole world" (v. 6).

"Bearing fruit and growing." The Gospel also bears fruit (v. 6). The Colossians passage assures us wherever "this Gospel" goes in the world, it produces godly fruit. When we share the Gospel, we can expect it will bear fruit. People will begin a personal relationship with Jesus. In the natural, good seeds planted in cultivated soil grow and spread. The empty ground covers with fruit-bearing growth. In the natural, seed planting combined with vision and care produces a predictable harvest. So it should be spiritually. When we share the principles of God's Word, we plant spiritual seeds. In the same way, we watch new life sprouting and flourishing.

"Just as it has been doing among you." Early Christianity produced a somewhat predictable and exciting pattern. For example, there was growth, spreading the Gospel, and a fruit-producing atmosphere in the Colossians' lives. God worked through them to continue growth and expansion wherever they took the Gospel seed.

We can depend on this same pattern. The Great Commission commands us to spread the Gospel to all! Each church operates like a deliberate, organized farm, planting specific seeds in different parts of the property and producing crops in bountiful amounts. Over time, farmers increase their farm size and crops by clearing new land of trees, rocks, and other obstacles. The more diligent and far-reaching the efforts to clear land, prepare the soil, and plant seeds, the greater the crop production. In terms of the Gospel, the more places we share, the more churches we plant, the more people we connect to Jesus. And in the same way farmers harvest seeds and plant them elsewhere, we send people into other fields to plant and produce.

Just as a farmer owns a field, we cultivate our fields of spiritual influence. We can plant seeds with families, workplaces, schools, and organizations, along with the towns and cities we live in. In regard to a church, members equipped by leaders (Eph. 4) take seeds to their fields of influence to plant, produce fruit, and keep spreading the Gospel. However, we don't need to wait for "official training" to plant seeds.

Once people receive Jesus, they're immediately eligible to share the Good News with others. For many, the most evangelistic period occurs shortly after conversion. Passion and God's power override their lack of knowledge. We should work with these new believers to help them mature, but also encourage them to use their newfound faith in the field God gives to them.

"Since the day you heard it." The Gospel carries the instant power to affect change. Paul speaks of the Gospel producing fruit "since the day you heard it" (v. 6). Though maturity and transformation take time, initial change can be instant. God often produces some immediate changes which demonstrate His will and power. This helps to build confidence in new believers that God impacts and changes their lives.

In my life, I partied and drank on Saturday afternoon, gave my life to Christ on Sunday morning, and haven't tasted a drink since then, over eighteen years later. I instantly gave up over a ten-year lifestyle of drinking. Other areas in my life, such as personal relationships, needed time to change, but some fruit sprang up immediately.

From the day we hear it, the Gospel can powerfully change us. We can expect and promote instant transformation when we share God's Word in faith and power. We can praise God when we observe personal change in lives. This creates an atmosphere of expectation, helping along the discipleship process while creating a culture of ongoing evangelism. This makes church life and our relationship with Jesus exciting!

Receive, Grow, Give It Away

After we receive salvation, the next step is spiritual growth. Whether knowledge, truth, or power, we let it grow within us. Then like a tree with fruit, we give it away to others so they walk in this ongoing process. The change we experience can attract others to want Jesus for themselves.

To give people a reason to become Christians, we model how Christ changes lives. Personal experience is key to understanding and sharing God's goodness. In many ways, we cannot passionately share something unless we know and understand it for ourselves. God's grace by definition seems unexplainable. But we can exhibit it by accepting God's forgiveness when we don't deserve it (Eph. 2:8-9), and gaining His strength and ability to do things we couldn't accomplish in our own strength.

Forgiveness when we don't deserve it and power to do what we're incapable of on our own. This is good stuff! People will notice.

Scripture also tells us to "grow in the grace and knowledge of our Lord and Savior Jesus Christ" (2 Pet. 3:18). Beyond the grace of salvation, there is a level of grace beyond the average Christian's experience and understanding. It connects with knowing God in deeper ways over time.

Growing deeper allows us to understand and experience God's grace in greater ways. I imagine the Christians Gandhi referred to were immature in their faith and character, not growing to be Christlike. As God's Word deepens in our souls, we grow more sensitive to the Holy Spirit. The closer we draw to Jesus, the more we become like Him. The heart of Jesus serves, seeks, and saves the lost. As we spend time with Him, we develop a greater love for the lost. We begin to understand God extends His grace to all, and He helps us reach the lost and share the Good News with them.

Give Somebody a Reason

As my friend Bob said, "Give somebody a reason to be a Christian." Everyday people radically transformed demonstrates God's power and ability to change lives. Changed people are often the clearest "reason" for others to follow Jesus. The angry, frustrated, and broken become happy, joyful, peaceful, and healed. This speaks volumes to lost and hurting people. Let's love people and share truth. When people receive it, let's send them into their "fields" so the process continues. We've got a reason for our voices to be heard.

CHAPTER 14

The Importance of Relationshpis

"I tried to share Jesus and it didn't work."

This conclusion can keep many Christians from sharing again. They overlook that evangelism usually needs time and ongoing relationships. Sometimes a one-time encounter results in salvation, but usually people don't want to feel rushed. They need to build trust and understand the concepts.

Imagine a stranger walking up with a big smile and asking for a date. Most people would say no just on the principle that they don't know the stranger. It would probably be foolish to say yes without at least some investigation. Is this person the right kind of "date material" or just plain crazy? In the same way, people need time to know us and consider our spiritual claims before they follow Christ. In response, we can engage them in pre-evangelism.

Let's define evangelism as sharing the Good News, the nuts

and bolts about sin, repentance, and commitment to Jesus. Pre-evangelism involves the conversations, issues, incidents, and relationships before people may be ready to grasp or accept spiritual concepts and make decisions for Christ. One reason Christians don't experience greater success in evangelism stems from rushing and forcing decisions. If people don't get time to process spiritual truths, they might reject the Gospel. Not because they don't want to connect with Jesus; they simply don't understand the Gospel yet.

In my experience, I embarked on a spiritual journey that took several years and many experiences before I'd hear a Gospel presentation. I had little sense of God, the Bible, or an eternal purpose. Or at least not anything resembling true Christianity. I sensed an answer "out there," but I didn't think it had anything to do with the Bible or Jesus. I had no mental framework that God could make a difference in my daily life. In my world, God didn't matter to me and I thought I didn't matter to Him. Praise God I was wrong!

Making a Difference Today

We're surrounded by people searching for God. They might read New Age books, or look to "experts," but still feel an internal void only God can fill. We might not be able to help someone complete their spiritual journey today, but we can succeed in encouraging them to take one step closer to Jesus.

Whether the process takes a day or ten years will not matter in eternity, so we can clear the way for people. The chart below is the Redmond Scale, presenting a spiritual progression of where people land in the pre-evangelism and evangelism process. We often get frustrated when we don't see people commit to Jesus after just a few conversations. Even though we don't want to turn evangelism into a formula, this chart can help us understand the stages seekers move through over time. Please notice that included in this diagram are religious people who are distant from Christ. We must remember that it doesn't matter how religious someone is, we are saved by grace through faith (Eph. 2:8-9). I am in no way saying these people are bad or immoral or that Christians are in any way better, simply that they are distant from having a personal relationship with Jesus.

Redmond Scale

REDMOND SCALE

of the Evangelism Journey

The Redmond Scale describes general categories and possible feelings of people who are disconnected from Jesus. The role of the Christ follower is to walk with people on a journey to Jesus. On that journey, people must overcome or resolve different feelings, gain knowledge, correct wrong knowledge, and possibly overcome negative religious experiences. Though salvation happens in a moment, there is most often a process to get to that point.

(continued on next page)

- 7	Anti-God	Atheistic with a strong anti-religious or anti-God philosophy and negative emotions towards God or religion. Feel that belief in God or religion is a bad thing that represents foolishness or deception.
- 6	Atheistic	Belief that God is not real, but with little or no strong emotional bias against God or religion. View God as a fairytale or creation of man.
- 5	Disinterested	Religion or God is not part of regular life. They are fine if others want to be religious, but they have no interest in God or religion. May have a vague belief in God but no real understanding of commitment to God or religion.
- 4	Religious or "Spiritual"	Committed to a religion, spirituality, or philosophy other than Christ. This can include religions such as Judaism, Islam, and Hinduism, and philosophies such as Buddhism, New Age, or Humanism. In a nutshell, they may be religious, "spiritual," or "believe in God," but they are purposely not committed to Christ with considerable barriers to Christ.

- 3	Curious	Can be from any background but have come to a place where they are investigating the claims of Christ and the Bible as a possibility in their life and as something special and different than their current understanding of God and religion. Starting to understand that sin is real and a problem in their life.
- 2	Want Relationship	Relationship now takes priority over religion, philosophy, and good works. They are disentangling from past emotional, situational, and intellectual thought processes and replacing them with Biblical thoughts and desires. Understand sin is a personal problem separating them from God.
- 1	Ready for Christ	Have investigated the claims of Christ and are ready to embrace them. They have worked through barrier questions and rejected other spiritual and philosophical options. Now understand they are a sinner in need of a Savior.
0	Salvation/ New Life	True repentance of sin takes place, faith is placed in Jesus, and the work of the cross and a commitment to follow Jesus takes place. This is the starting line of a personal relationship with Jesus and the Christian life.

The Journey to Jesus

Some people are purposely distant from God by choice. Others may be religious but committed to a faith or philosophy that doesn't see Jesus as Lord and Savior. Still others may be indifferent, actively searching, or even ready to begin a personal relationship with Jesus. Our goal is to walk with them so that over time, they keep taking steps closer to Jesus. The Apostle James wrote, "Come near to God and he will come near to you" (James 4:8). When we get closer to God, He rewards us by drawing closer. Pre-evangelism allows time and space for people to move toward Jesus.

When we understand the stages of people's spiritual journeys, we can walk with friends, family, and coworkers with patience. This chart can pinpoint "where people are" and help us pray for them. Keep in mind every step is progress and success.

In my speaking experiences, I've asked people in churches, "If it took twenty years to win someone to Jesus, would it be too long?"

I've gotten funny reactions and faces from the crowd. The general sentiment reveals twenty years is a ridiculously long time to win someone to Jesus.

I then ask, "Is there anyone in your life you've known for over twenty years who doesn't know Jesus?"

The hands go up all over the room and faces begin to smile.

I then ask, "Would it be worth the time if those people gave their lives to Jesus after twenty years?" Heads nod with understanding.

A close friend of mine has led many people to Jesus. He's gifted at helping church-going people who've never made a personal commitment to Jesus. To know him now, he's a faithful husband and strong member of our church. But for many years, he lived a sinful life while still attending church every Sunday. He was a heavy drinker, a drug user for some time, an adulterer for years, and a drug dealer for a while. He had knowledge, but didn't surrender his life to Jesus until his late thirties. Despite all of these behaviors, he was a committed church goer every Sunday!

I can't answer why some come to the Lord quickly and others take years. But I'm glad people didn't give up on my friend, and neither did God. I can share many similar stories. We probably all know people that could take years to connect with Jesus. We can't control the timing but can affect "being heard" through our words and actions. We may not engage in perfect conversations that convince them to recognize their sinful ways, but we can consistently move them toward repentance.

In the Meantime

When people recognize Jesus in us, it can spark spiritual hunger in them. We need to spend time and enjoy them "as they are," and not just treat them as evangelism projects.

In the meantime, we can pray and ask God for a strategy. Is it best to confront or to just be positive and pray? Different situations require different approaches. This returns to the Holy Spirit leading us.

Also, don't let people's spiritual decisions create relational rifts because of their choices. However, God doesn't call us to be abused or a doormat to win them to Him. At times, walking away may be needed for them to seriously look at themselves. But no matter the situation with one person, maintain other healthy and life-giving relationships. Never forget God promises peace even in difficult situations.

Remember what the baseball player Yogi Berra said: "It ain't over 'til it's over!"

Many people pray and share with friends and family for years and some people don't respond until on their deathbeds. It's a shame some people stay so hard hearted, it takes their own inevitable death to soften them. Thankfully, if approaching death wakes people up spiritually, if they receive God's grace, they will live in heaven for eternity. Even if they wasted this life, eternity with God in heaven will be worth our prayers and efforts. It's never too late to let our voices be heard!

CHAPTER 15

Overcoming Our Feelings

I remember a phone call from a college student who had a new roommate. The student was wrestling with a dream she'd had and how she should respond to it. I clearly thought God wanted her to connect the roommate with Jesus, but I could tell a roadblock stood in the way.

It began with a "Can I talk to you?" question. She dreamed her roommate was in danger and needed to escape their dorm room. In the dream, the student tried to get her roommate to climb out the window to safety, but she wouldn't. When the student finally convinced her roommate to climb out the window, the dream returned them to their dorm room. The danger still existed and they needed to get out again.

The dream confused and bothered my college friend, especially because it became a dream within a dream and repeated itself. She'd been calling me for two days to talk about it.

At first, I laughed. I was at work and my mind focused elsewhere. I wasn't expecting a phone call with a request to interpret a dream.

As we talked, I asked about the roommate. What was she like? What was their relationship like?

The girls had been roommates for several months; cordial but not overly social. They felt more like accidental roommates than close friends, due to different personalities more than anything else. The student described her roommate as a nice girl with some religious background, but definitely not someone who knew and served Jesus. In short, she was a hardworking, nice person, but was disconnected from Jesus.

As we talked, my college friend wanted an answer to the dream's meaning. To me, it seemed clear. First, her roommate was in trouble, and second, God wanted to use her to help the roommate.

My college friend felt burdened from this dream, but couldn't put her finger on the reason. So I asked, "Does your roommate know Jesus?"

She said the roommate owned a statue of the Virgin Mary and prayed sometimes, but probably didn't know Jesus personally. Then the light bulb turned on. I simply stated the obvious, "God wants to use you to win her to Jesus."

Her response was instant and sincere: "Who am I to tell people about Jesus? I'm struggling myself." Emotionally, she disqualified herself from sharing her faith.

She added, "I am still learning myself, I still mess up." She probably thought, *Why can't God send someone else, you know, someone better?*

I responded simply. "No one is perfect. God doesn't need a perfect vessel to work through, simply a willing vessel." I paused and added, "God could send anyone to share Jesus, but you're her roommate."

The Ministry of Presence

In regard to evangelism, a roommate, friend, or family member allows us to participate in the ministry of presence. We are with them day in and day out. When good things happen, we can celebrate. When struggles or disappointments descend, we can listen and encourage. Our presence is an open door to say, do, and learn things others can't access.

Ongoing presence in people's lives can create a bridge to their thoughts, feelings, and beliefs. This can happen whether someone is a roommate for a few months, a coworker, a long-term friend, or a family member. During the seasons of life, a level of trust can develop that can't build from a casual connection. Many times, more than the right answers, people just want someone with them.

Despite a relationship with the roommate, my college friend still felt she wasn't "good enough" to share Christ. In my mind, she was perfect for the job. I encouraged her and explained God just needs a willing person. I said, "If your roommate points out your faults, just agree and say, 'I'm not perfect and that's why I need a savior, too.'"

Interestingly, I'd known this college student for close to ten years. Of thousands of teens I'd worked with, she was absolutely one of the best. In terms of dedication, growth, and loving the Lord, she was amazing and doing awesome work in college. Even with these qualities, she felt inadequate. In my mind, if she felt not good enough, then who was? This young lady was a role model for others, but she still struggled and felt insufficient to share the Gospel. I encouraged her to not focus on being perfect, but just let Jesus use her to do His will.

Nice People on the Wrong Road

My friend's roommate represented many people today. For the most part, our society is full of "nice" people who mean well. I've met few people who were deliberately mean or evil, but the majority of people are usually nice and well-meaning for most of their lives. They have moments of sin which disrupt their lives, and even those around them. But they think if they're nice more than bad, they're okay. They hope their "niceness" outweighs their mistakes so they earn a good shot at making it to heaven.

Sometimes telling a "nice person" they're on the wrong road—the road to hell—feels unsettling. Being nice doesn't get us into heaven and being bad (sinning) doesn't keep us out. Sin separates us from God and creates a distance from Him. But this separation can be removed by putting our faith in Jesus and the work of the

Cross. Doing good things and being nice are great, but they can't earn our way to heaven. Only the forgiveness of sin through God's grace makes entry into heaven possible (Eph. 2:8-9).

People We Don't Like

As the conversation with my young collegian progressed, another roadblock sprang up. She shared one of her feelings about her roommate: "I don't like her!"

My initial response was simple, "So?"

The roommates' personalities and life directions were different. They'd offended each other. I told her, "Sinners sin. It's what they do."

Looking back, it sounds insensitive but in the realm of eternity, we can't let feelings block helping people connect with Jesus. We can grab the remote control and ignore the person sitting across the room, like a modern-day Jonah. But running away didn't work for the prophet. It probably won't work for us, either.

Christ followers travel one road. Those disconnected from Christ travel an opposite road. Christ died for us to switch roads. As Christ followers we're to lay down our lives and help people make this change, too. People like the roommate act worldly and this can offend us, but Christ never let sin stop Him from loving someone. Connecting people with Jesus is not a matter of doing what we want, but what God wants. Did Jesus feel like being beaten and crucified? Whatever we feel in terms of discomfort or being disliked doesn't compare to what Jesus suffered.

I explained to my college friend that people act the way they do because they don't know Jesus. Only Jesus can change them. If we wait for them to change first, we probably won't connect them with Jesus. The Lord purposefully sought the sick and sinful (Matt. 9:12), and later He sent the Holy Spirit to help us share His message (Acts 1:8).

Catching a Fish Before We Clean It

An old proverb says we can't clean a fish before we catch it. Until that fish lays in the boat or on land, it's impossible to clean it. When we clean a fish, we remove all the scales, internal organs, waste, and anything else we don't want to eat. Basically, we get rid of the bad or useless parts. Looking at this from a spiritual viewpoint, we can't clean up people's behaviors and habits until they're in God's Kingdom and He begins to "clean them up."

If people don't deal with their basic and root issues, we can't expect the outside or superficial things to change. We often focus on people's outward actions caused by sin. Their nasty attitudes, bad habits, and purposely sinful lifestyles bother us. We try to encourage or "guilt" them into changing without getting to the root issue. When describing people's sins and weaknesses, I hear Christians say, "They know better" or, "I told them but they didn't listen!" The reality is they're separated from God and the "things of God" make no sense to them. "The person without the Spirit does not accept the things that come from the Spirit of God but considers them foolishness, and cannot understand them because they are discerned only through the Spirit" (1 Cor. 2:14).

This scripture helped me immensely when I became frustrated with the behavior of certain people. I tried to teach spiritual things to unspiritual people. This verse teaches us that people not born again and without the Holy Spirit can't understand biblical truth. It's foolishness to them. What seems like common sense and simple to us, seems like nonsense to them.

Certain things can only be understood through the Holy Spirit. Imagine taking people who never left their hometown and dropping them off in a foreign country where they never heard the local language. Of course we wouldn't expect them to understand the locals. We often do something similar when we take people from our culture, drop them into a church, and speak Christianese to them. They're baffled by our strange language and customs.

Identifying the reasons for people's behavior and their lack of understanding can help us set aside negative feelings and replace them with patience and love. We can better learn how to communicate and still let our voices be heard.

CHAPTER 16

Speaking Words of Life

As the conversation continued with my college friend, I asked why she hadn't led her roommate to Jesus. She answered, "I don't know what to say."

I was floored! *You don't know what to say? You don't know the words to lead someone to Jesus? Really?*

At first, my pride was probably the biggest casualty. This was one of "my kids," who grew up in my church. She was a role model to other teens and didn't know what to say? How could she not know? She had more passion for Jesus than most teens or adults. I'd assumed she had the words, but I was wrong.

It felt painfully obvious I'd given this young woman principles to change her own life, but didn't help her internalize how to share them with others. I'd failed to teach her what to say in a way she understood it.

I am huge on evangelism and in my mind have taught it a thousand times. But this struck me: as church leaders and individual followers of Christ, we must purposely learn and share the words of life to connect people to Jesus. People spend their entire lives in churches, know Jesus personally, but can't communicate words of life to others. If this young woman didn't have the words, then how many others don't? The state of the Body of Christ hit me. This was one of the reasons so many Christians don't lead someone to Jesus. They don't know what to say.

Words of Eternal Life

When many of Jesus' followers deserted Him, He asked the disciples if they would leave Him, too. Simon Peter answered him, "Lord, to whom shall we go? You have the words of eternal life" (John 6:68). Jesus shared the words of eternal life and as His followers, we can, too.

This is not the first time someone I'd worked with for years didn't understand how to express the Gospel. When I took two teen boys to Billy Graham's final crusade in New York City, I told them about the evangelist's history, his calling to preach, and how he shared the Gospel with millions. One of the young men looked at me and asked, "How does someone get to heaven?" On the outside I remained calm and smiled, but on the inside I screamed, *"WHAT???"* If someone had turned my internal emotional reaction into a movie clip, it would probably have shown me smashing something!

These young men heard the Gospel explained many times,

but didn't have the words to explain how sinners live separated from God. They couldn't explain that Jesus died on the Cross for our sin. That we must put our faith in the work of the Cross and choose to follow Jesus. That when we repent, God forgives sin and we begin a new life with Jesus as Lord and Savior. Years of hearing the Gospel for themselves didn't establish these principles in their minds for them to share with others. I know they understood spiritually, and I'd seen their conversion and transformation. They understood for themselves, but didn't know the words to share with others.

The Gospel in a Nutshell

I was much better at helping people connect with Jesus than equipping them to share Him with others. This punched me in my emotional gut! In response, I developed a short list of principles to help people know and express the Gospel. The goal wasn't to memorize a process, but to internalize the principles and share them in normal conversations, either one piece at a time or as one complete story. In "Bridging the Gap between Man and God," I listed these principles and Bible verses.

1. **God wants an eternal relationship with you.**

   Ephesians 1:17 — "So that you may know him better."

   Colossians 1:16, KJV — "All things were created by him [Jesus] and for him."

2. **Our wrong choices (sin) have broken this relationship.**

   Romans 3:23 — "All have sinned and fall short of the

glory of God."

Romans 6:23a — "The wages of sin is death." This means separation.

Isaiah 59:2 — "But your iniquities have separated you from your God."

3. **Jesus is the bridge back to this relationship.**

   John 14:6 — "Jesus answered, 'I am the way and the truth and the life. No one comes to the Father except through me.'"

   Romans 6:23b — "But the gift of God is eternal life in Christ Jesus our Lord."

   John 5:24 — "I tell you the truth, whoever hears my word and believes him who sent me has eternal life and will not be condemned; he has crossed over from death to life."

4. **We must choose and be loyal to this relationship.**

   John 1:12 — "Yet to all who did receive him, to those who believed in his name, he gave the right to become children of God."

   John 15:13-14 — "Greater love has no one than this: to lay down one's life for his friends. You are my friends if you do what I command."

I've deliberately shared these principles in a conversational way and also as a systematic list. The Good News is most often shared best in conversations, especially when shared outside the church. Memorizing verses can help internalize the principles for use in conversations. Unfortunately, memorization isn't a habit for most people.

How many times in school did we study for a test, take the exam, and never think about the information again? We can treat the Bible like this. We absorb the Gospel long enough to apply it to choosing Jesus, but then forget enough to make us ineffective or a non-participator in the Great Commission. We often define a "good" or "healthy" church as lots of people with an exciting atmosphere, instead of by the spiritual health or evangelistic passion of the members.

Who has the biggest church? Who is the most popular preacher? These are the wrong questions to ask. Christianity began with one man and twelve friends living together and serving and sharing with others. For hundreds of years, Christianity was only a face-to-face, relational religion. Now in our results-driven society, the bigger, better, and faster often rule. While I believe many large churches are ordained by God and do amazing things, they are only truly successful if they win souls, make disciples, and serve others where they live and hurt. This is the job of Christ's followers.

Face-to-Face and Door-to-Door

We often neglect the power of basic Christianity. We downplay the power of the unknown Christian reaching and serving others when no one watches. Because we're a results-driven society, we often define Christianity by the loudest, smoothest, most impressive speakers. This results in many Christians feeling like they don't measure up, and they don't have the right or ability to lead others to Jesus. This is a lie!

God uses us anywhere as we are. The cumulative effects of unknown Christ followers outweigh those of the greatest public preacher. We need to share the Gospel as often and in as many ways as possible. If each one of us does what God calls us to do, we can fulfill His will. We can't worry about who we are not, or what we can't do. We're to get busy doing what we can do now.

On our own, we are inadequate, unworthy, and unable. But through Christ, we are adequate (Isa. 53:5); worthy (Rom. 5:19); and able (Phil. 4:13). Christ loves us as we are and uses us where we are. Yes, we need to continually repent, grow, and change, but if God must wait for perfection, He could never use us.

We're created to know Christ and make Him known to others. It's been said Christianity is "one beggar giving another beggar a piece of bread." Christians are no better than anyone else. If it seems like they are, it's because God changed them from who they used to be.

It's all about serving God. We live for the purposes bigger than ourselves. We must let our voices be heard.

CHAPTER 17

Defeating the Enemy Called Fear

The writer Mark Twain claimed, "Courage is resistance to fear, mastery of fear—not absence of fear."[5] For many, fear is the greatest obstacle to sharing the Gospel. Low-level fear causes people to hesitate. High-level fear can lead to total shutdowns. Whatever our level of fear we must consider it a spiritual enemy.

Actually, as followers of Christ, we're in a spiritual war with many enemies. "For our struggle is not against flesh and blood, but against the rulers, against the authorities, against the powers of this dark world and against the spiritual forces of evil in the heavenly realms" (Eph. 6:12). In addition to these dark forces, we also encounter internal enemies battering our emotions. Fear is such an enemy, sent to disrupt God's plan. At the same time, the Bible assures us fear doesn't originate with God. In a letter to Timothy, the Apostle Paul wrote, "For God did not give us a spirit of fear, but of power and of love and of a sound mind"

(2 Tim.1:7, NKJV).

God doesn't give us a spirit of fear. So if we're sharing our faith, we don't want fear. If it's not from God, it's either sent from the enemy of our souls, Satan, and his kingdom, or it arises from our own flesh. Either way, we don't want to entertain it.

Anything and everything from Satan's kingdom is our enemy and the harsher we deal with it, the better. Often we're too nice or passive when under spiritual attack.

Our Flesh and Fear

Fear can rise up from our own personal issues. Lack of confidence, past failure, and low self-esteem can all contribute. But when talking about the Gospel, we're not to share "in the flesh." Without the Holy Spirit, our efforts can't win souls. Fear causes actual physiological changes such as increased blood pressure, release of hormones, anxiety, and other problems. Fear hinders and debilitates. People respond in different ways to fear and the physical and emotional manifestations it produces. It can be like brakes on a car. It can slow us down or bring us to a complete stop. It just depends on how hard we press down on the brakes.

For most people, fear pops up its ugly head somewhere in their soul-winning efforts. The question is: will we entertain fear or chop off its head? Too many people treat fear like the family dog who belongs in the kitchen, instead of a rattlesnake that slithered in. The dog is a family member, always around and we regularly interact with it. Sometimes it's a hassle, and may be an inconvenience at times, but it's part of family life.

Too many people accept fear as a normal part of life rather than something to recognize, overcome, and eliminate. Imagine finding a rattlesnake in the kitchen. Would we let it hang out for dinner or make sure it left dead? Would we snuggle up to it or cut off its head? I imagine we would do everything possible to eliminate its presence!

Love, Power, and Authority

The cure to overcoming fear depends on walking in God's love, power, and authority. "There is no fear in love. But perfect love drives out fear" (1 John 4:18a). When we walk in God's love, we're filled with love, comfort, and peace. We also walk in the power of the Holy Spirit. When these work together, they can drive out fear.

Just like driving out that rattlesnake, we need to drive out fear. We might say, "I'm not messing with a rattlesnake on my own!" I have good news. God doesn't expect us to drive out fear in our strength and ability, but in His.

Several years ago, I was on a sabbatical and passing through the worst trial of my life. During this time, I took a thirteen-mile hike. It was in the fall so I finished hiking in the dark. The last part of the trail incorporated pavement so I knew I wouldn't get lost. That was the plan, but I still walked in what felt like "the middle of nowhere" for a couple of hours. It felt like the darkness in my life.

For the first time, I was caught in several difficult situations I had no control over. I was at the mercy of several people whom

I couldn't trust. As I walked, I was consumed with pain and fear, but I knew I could trust God. I looked up at the sky and the countless stars, and the scripture burst into my spirit: "He determines the number of the stars and calls them each by name" (Ps. 147:4).

As I looked up at the vast sky, it reminded me of God's greatness. He knows every star. He actually named each one and calls it by name! When that revelation hit, fear left and peace washed over me. I'd hiked miles into the woods on my own, but I knew God watched over me and would take care of me. That night, in the worst season of my life, God's love drove out the pain and consuming fear controlling me. He didn't leave me in my limitations, but helped me walk in His love, power, and authority.

Limited on Our Own

Fear is a natural reaction when we rely on our own ability, but when God strengthens our inner being, we change. Paul prayed, "I pray that out of his glorious riches he may strengthen you with power through his Spirit in your inner being" (Eph. 3:16). With this strengthening, we can do all things through Christ's strength (Phil. 4:13), including winning souls. We're set free to share Christ with boldness. Just as God's perfect love drives out our fear, we can share God's love so others can be set free of their fear.

Our culture teaches us to be proud, strong, and self-sufficient. Fear emerges when we realize we can't live up to these impossible standards every moment of the day. But God works differently. He "opposes the proud but shows favor to the humble" (Jas 4:6).

I've heard grace defined as God's enabling power to be what He has called us to be and to do what He has called us to do.

When we reach the end of ourselves, we are often just starting to touch the will and power of God. Jesus said to Paul, "My grace is sufficient for you, for my power is made perfect in weakness." The apostle responded, "Therefore I will boast all the more gladly about my weaknesses, so that Christ's power may rest on me" (2 Cor. 12:9).

Paul also wrote, "The weakness of God is stronger than human strength" (1 Cor.1:25b). He used a hyperbole, a deliberate exaggeration, to make a point. God has no weaknesses. But if He did, His worst weakness would be stronger than our greatest strength.

Spiritual strength also results from our own efforts. The greatest factor of spiritual growth is having a daily quiet time. When we study God's Word, pray, and spend time with our Lord, we gain strength and confidence. Like a weightlifter gains strength over time, a daily quiet time is our spiritual gym that builds us up.

Building Confidence to Witness

When we understand we don't need to function in our strength, but instead, in God's strength, this releases pressure. We can't, but He can! Fear diminishes because our confidence and ability relies on an all-powerful, all-knowing, all-loving God. We team up with Him to do what He already wants to accomplish.

Imagine having a multi-billionaire friend who asks us to help him pick out a summer cottage that costs $200,000. We know he will pay for it with cash. He just wants help finding a home. Would we feel pressure to pay for the cottage ourselves? Would we feel inadequate because we don't have the money? Of course not. We would rely on our friend to pay, and in the meantime, enjoy the house-hunting task.

In the same way, when winning souls, Jesus already paid the cost. He wants us to come along and win souls. This is the type of confidence we can enjoy. His power and ability, combined with our effort to co-labor, results in souls entering His Kingdom. Just take one step at a time, walking forward with Jesus.

Every summer, our family goes to an amusement park called Great Adventure. Two summers ago, instead of our whole family going, I just took my two middle-school daughters. In one day, I rode more roller coasters than I had in my entire life. I sat down, stood up, hung with my feet dangling, and laid on my stomach to imitate Superman. I rode forward and backward. I flipped and looped. Although I looked brave, I started out fearful. But repetition made the rides more comfortable. With practice, fear became less and I embarked on bigger and faster coasters. I felt most of my fear leading up to a ride, but once I buckled in and took off, I loved it. I actually started looking forward to the next ride.

I draw parallels between my roller-coaster day and sharing our faith. For me, the worst part of the roller-coaster experience was standing in line. I waited and stared at this huge structure reaching into the sky. The coaster plummeted up and down, adding in twists, turns, and loops. This can feel like the moments before sharing our faith. We look at this intimidating task and question if we really want to do it.

The next frightening part was ascending the first hill. The click, click, click of the coaster as it ascended and the anticipation as it slowly prepared to descend could unnerve me. This can represent the beginning of a Christ-sharing conversation. It can be awkward. We don't know what will happen, but it will be something out of the norm.

Once the coaster dropped, the fear and questioning turned into exhilaration. This often happens in our conversations as initial fear and anxiety disappear, and the interaction becomes a fun time sharing our personal experiences, along with God's love and plans.

Although I enjoyed myself on each coaster ride, when I got ready for the next one, sometimes I'd question whether I wanted to risk it again. To me, this demonstrates the emotional reality of sharing our faith. Even though confidence grows over time, it doesn't mean we'll never feel fear or anxiety again. We want and love to share, but this doesn't mean we won't question our abilities or wrestle with our emotions.

A popular slogan encourages us to "Feel the fear and do it anyway." We can feel the fear, but still let our voices be heard.

CHAPTER 18

Winning Souls, Not Arguments

In our family, we call my wife the Queen of Seasoning. Coming from a Jamaican background, serving plain food to someone would be an insult. It also would be a poor representation of her. It would just be wrong!

To my wife, every time she adds a seasoning, this demonstrates caring about someone. It also exhibits holding herself to a high standard, ensuring she gives someone the best she can. For me and my love of food, this is wonderful! I know no matter what arrives on the dinner table, it will taste good. We're often invited to barbecues due to her legendary baked beans.

We can bake a piece of chicken and serve it overcooked, dry, and with no flavor. Or we can slow cook that piece of chicken in a homemade sauce so we can cut it with a fork and it melts in the mouth. Either way, it's the same piece of chicken. The slow-cooked piece tastes fit for a king while the dried-up meat might be rejected by a dog. The only difference: the preparation and delivery of the chicken.

It's the same way with evangelism. I've addressed the preparation aspect; let's look at the delivery. While sharing the Gospel message, we continue relationships and sharing the truth in love. This is important because one of the greatest turnoffs to non-Christians is arrogant Christians telling the truth. Jesus came to seek and save the lost, not to win a debating contest. We share the truth in love and might be rejected over and over again. (At times, true victory can look like defeat in the world's eyes.) But it's not about us or the moment, it's about eternity. We soften the soil and sow lots of seeds through unconditional love before we actually reap fruit. Unfortunately, many Christians have been arrogant and more concerned about being right and sharing truth than effectively communicating the fullness of the Gospel.

Wisdom screams we need to place winning souls above feeling good about being right. An ancient proverb writer revealed, "The fruit of the righteous is a tree of life, and he who wins souls is wise" (Prov. 11:30). As Christ demonstrated, it's not about the one making the sacrifice, it's about the sacrificed One. Sharing the truth can be difficult at times, but we can interact to bring people to Jesus instead of driving them away.

Serving the Truth

When we share biblical principles and the Gospel, we tell the truth. In a sense, we feed people truth. We can deliver it dry, unseasoned, and hard to swallow, or well-seasoned so people want second and third servings. Although my wife doesn't share her secret recipes with everyone, God shares His "recipes" and the most important ingredient is love. Jesus declares He is the truth (John 14:6) and the Bible says God is love (1 John 4:8). So to communicate God, we must communicate love. The Apostle Paul wrote about "speaking the truth in love" to one another (Eph. 4:15, KJV). Love communicates the essence of God's nature.

God wants His people to exercise wisdom. It is greater than intelligence or knowledge. Wisdom is the ability to make good decisions in complicated or sensitive situations, resulting in desired outcomes. I'm not suggesting we water down the Gospel, but the communicator should be a bridge, not a roadblock.

Colossians 4:5-7 encourages Christians to "Be wise in the way you act toward outsiders; make the most of every opportunity. Let your conversation be always full of grace, seasoned with salt, so that you may know how to answer everyone."

Real Change Really Matters

Our culture often believes "being right" elevates us to a place of superiority. People argue, fuss, and fight to prove and justify their thoughts, beliefs, and actions. We often take great pride in proving others wrong. Just look at pop culture, talk shows, and news channels. Too often, the person who yells the loudest and longest is "the winner."

However, winning arguments doesn't necessarily translate into changed lives. God is more concerned about forgiven and regenerated souls than us being right. Arguing might work in the secular world when people just want to be heard, but it doesn't work when winning hearts and souls.

If we share the Bible in an accurate way, we are right—period. God's Word is truth, fact, and reality. It's never wrong because God isn't wrong. But we can be a different story. We can be wrong, unbalanced, or unloving when we share God's absolute love and truth. Even if we are accurate and correct, the manner in which we communicate God's message is important. When Jesus came to earth, He was full of "grace and truth" (John 1:17). Part of that truth includes God's grace that covers all sin if people will receive it.

Yes, there will be times we boldly stand up for what we believe and can't be moved. But most of the time we share faith and Christ's love, we speak in a conversational tone. During these times, we can walk in quiet confidence, knowing God does His work. As people submit their lives to the Almighty God, it's usually a quiet, internal process. We can't expect people to cry out loud, "What must I do to be saved?" (Acts 16:30) every time we engage in spiritual conversation. It may happen, but whether loud or quiet, it's the decision that matters.

Being Still While God Works

Part of the reason Christians sound offensive emerges from our brokenness and search for significance. We want to feel like we make a difference. While we're created to make a difference, the power of God working through our gifts and callings makes the true difference, not us. We contribute deliberate actions, but I've tried to get results through my own efforts and found out it wasn't me after all. I discovered when I relax and promote God, people will elevate Him. As God's Word says, "Be still, and know that I am God; I will be exalted among the nations, I will be exalted in the earth" (Ps. 46:10).

There is power when we understand we don't need to prove we're right. I've found one of the most powerful ways to influence people is to share the truth and then just love them. It is powerful when people reject or don't visibly accept the message and we still give them unconditional love. It speaks loudly when we care more about people than trying to get them to "be Christians." It demonstrates we care about them, no matter what they think or believe. We demonstrate God's unconditional love.

When I became our church's pastor for evangelism, in my first teaching to our church leadership team, I told the group our goal was to love and serve people. That's whether or not they begin a relationship with Jesus or ever join our church. I still firmly believe this.

Not Trying to Convince

I've discussed Christ with people and they push back; at times I don't respond or argue. Sometimes people are working through issues and they need time. Others are convinced religion or Christianity or faith are not real, or at least not for them. They reach this conclusion after years of negative experiences or a long spiritual-growth process. In an ongoing relationship, at times it's best to sow the seed and let it grow. Several times when sharing about God and His Word, people suddenly looked at me and said, "You're not trying to convince me!" I smiled and said, "I can't convince people, only God can." Their faces lit up when I said that.

Sometimes the best approach is to ask a question and let people talk. At times I ask, "Are you happy with the way things are going?" Or, "Do you ever feel like something is missing?" Then I wait for the response. People want to be heard and listening may go further than talking. This may take humility and patience on our part, but remember, we're called to wisdom.

But what happens when we share our faith and the arrogant or combative one sits across the table? We could encounter someone looking for a fight. This person isn't as much interested in finding the truth as in winning an argument. The interaction can posture like two arrogant peacocks with their feathers brightly displayed, battling and showing off for a female peacock. At times, after the two males exhaust themselves in their show of bravado, the lady peacock walks away, unimpressed by either show-off.

Many times, I've witnessed a Christian and non-Christian walking away from each other, both proud they made their points. No one was convinced of anything except their own beliefs. Both became more entrenched, one in their unbelief and the other in their superiority and pride of sharing the truth to the "lost one."

Remember Your Goal

Our goal is to win souls. Whether loud or soft, quickly or over the years, what matters is connecting people to Jesus. Scripture says "today is the day of salvation" (2 Cor. 6:2) and we should try to win people to Jesus today. Even if it takes years or decades for some, we can get started today. Who can we smile at? With whom can we demonstrate God's love? Who might respond to a scripture or biblical principle? What we can't do shouldn't get in the way of what we can do.

Share the truth in love. Walk in love even when it's not received. God's power is released in our humility. Sow seeds and be still because God works behind the scenes, in the souls and minds of people we love and connect with each day. I'm convinced the Great Commission will not be fulfilled by people with microphones in their hands, but by an army of nameless Christians who simply love Jesus and want to share Him with others. Everyday people who do their part and let their voices be heard.

PART FOUR

Fulfilling the Great Commission

CHAPTER 19

Not Pulpit-Driven Only

What if every day someone from a local church reported a new Christ follower? How much joy would the congregation feel if every Sunday seven new faces appeared in the service? What if families attended together because every member served Jesus? Imagine the fun of greeting people from your neighborhood or community added to the local church every week. It'd feel like the early church, when souls were added daily to the fellowship (Acts 2:47).

This scenario isn't the norm and won't happen by accident. For the Body of Christ to truly embrace the Great Commission, pastors must drive it from the pulpit in greater ways. God established ministry leaders to equip their churches to minister. "So Christ himself gave the apostles, the prophets, the evangelists, the pastors and teachers, to equip his people for works of service, so that the body of Christ may be built up" (Eph. 4:11-12). Preaching from the pulpit, teaching a Sunday school class, or leading a small group equips the congregation to do ministry. As this equipping builds soul winners, more people will connect to Jesus.

Although Christ intended all believers to embrace the Great Commission, over time, ministry shifted to a few. For the first three centuries of the church, the predominant culture was that every Christ follower was a minister of the gospel. There was a major shift after Christianity became the official religion of the Roman Empire and clergy assumed control. Today we enjoy freedom, but many in the pulpit don't understand the need or feel hesitant to put demands on congregants for soul winning. In many churches, the main focus turns into caring for the existing flock. But Jesus and the early church focused on taking care of the existing believers, plus winning new souls. In short, many in the pulpit don't effectively teach and equip their congregation to take on Christ's priority: to seek and save the lost!

In my travels, pastors often ask me to plant seeds, to build their congregation's faith for sharing Christ. I frequently speak on personal evangelism and many in the congregation respond like it's the first time they've seriously considered personally sharing Christ with others. Faith comes by hearing God's Word (Rom. 10:17), and if we want people to win souls, we must teach them soul-winning scriptures.

Building an Evangelistic Church

Regarding evangelism, the American Church is a sleeping giant. God wants to waken it to bring the Gospel to the ends of the earth. It's possible to reach the world if pulpits across the nation would proclaim the need for every Christian to win souls. Aside from pastors and leaders, countless others can teach personal evangelism, too. Laypeople could actually focus more on evangelism, allowing God to use them in great ways.

Based on a biblical pattern, when God wants to reach a group of people with a message, He first speaks to their leaders. Leaders then preach this vision, and hearers must listen, receive, and do. With time and teaching, pastors and leaders can build an evangelistic congregation. They can pursue the following approaches:

1. Preaching about evangelism. When a pastor preaches on a specific topic, it tends to build faith in that area. So it's important evangelism starts from the pulpit. If the pastor does not passionately equip a congregation on evangelism, people will not build the faith to lead people to Jesus. Studying and memorizing key scriptures can also motivate congregants toward sharing Christ.

2. Establishing soul winning as a priority. People respond to a message from the pulpit when it's established as a priority. Research reveals people are more prone to join churches that put demands on them. They want to join something that makes a difference. Leaders can keep spectator Christians happy by not challenging them, but will find it difficult to reach the unchurched and build larger or stronger churches. Challenge church people to evangelize!

3. Teaching and demonstrating approaches. In my church, most often we teach and encourage conversational evangelism.

This involves bringing spiritual and biblical principles into everyday conversations. We also introduce evangelism into our weekend services, small groups, and special events. In addition, some members participate in street evangelism, beginning conversations with strangers. While street evangelism is effective for some, it shouldn't be the only way to share Christ. Different methods prove effective for different personality types.

4. Modeling personal evangelism. Pastors and leaders can model evangelism not just from pulpits, but also in their personal lives. Church leaders can set the pace for connecting people to Jesus. They can inspire congregants toward reaching outside the church to win the lost. Even when a church begins to emphasize evangelism, the people still need to learn by example.

5. Training opportunities. To overcome a lack of experience, a church can offer different types of training. At my church we train people with a thirty-minute session entitled, "Sharing Your Story." This interactive conversation explains how anyone can share a few simple experiences and help others think about where God stands in their lives. We also hold a School of Evangelism with three-hour workshops about sharing personal stories, intertwined with the Gospel. We also form small groups focused on training and doing face-to-face evangelism. As a church, we believe our greatest tool of evangelism is our people. We meet people "where they are" and help them grow. We can't assume people "get it" and just naturally help others connect with Jesus. The statistics and history prove otherwise.

Making Wrong Assumptions

Before I accepted Christ as my personal Savior, I sat in religious services where I didn't understand the symbolism of certain actions and ceremonies. I wasn't against God, I just couldn't understand Him beyond a religious ceremony that didn't change my life. Yet leaders in the church and my family thought I understood.

Similar to my experience, we can assume because we live in a "Christian" nation, people hear and understand the Gospel of salvation through Jesus Christ. But often, like me, they don't understand at all. That's why Americans often reject religion. In their minds religion, the Easter bunny, and Santa Claus belong in the same category. So after childhood, why bother?

Consequently, people may ignore Jesus, and in the afterlife live separated from God. For most people, this isn't an act of deliberate rebellion against God. They just didn't know or understand. This happens all over the world, and maybe with the family next door, or our coworkers.

For all of us, spiritual beliefs develop through a lifelong series of events and experiences. Some key moments significantly impact us, but most spiritual growth results from many small steps adding up over time. Similarly, each day we can grow in understanding the importance of winning souls. Growing in confidence and the leading of the Holy Spirit matures over time.

If church members only observe evangelism on Sunday mornings, this can also set up false assumptions. When listeners respond and accept Jesus, congregants only see the moment of surrender. This can lead to the belief we just talk to people once and they accept salvation. This sets up unrealistic expectations. It can also make believers feel like failures when they try to lead people to Christ and these listeners aren't ready.

People develop belief systems based on years of teachings and experiences. When we present the Gospel, we're asking them to reject old beliefs and accept new ones. We're asking them to trust the unknown. Most often, a process brings them home to Jesus.

The Way Back Home

When I ride my bike or jog, I move straight in one direction. If I want to guarantee a certain distance or exercise level, I go to a location and then return the same way. I'm usually enthusiastic about the trip, but eventually boredom or fatigue kicks in. The real workout isn't the trip to my destination; it's the way back. I run or cycle in one direction away from home because it forces me to return at the same distance.

For most people without a personal relationship with Jesus, they've steadily walked away from Jesus. Their thoughts and actions move them away from God, their spiritual home. Just like my exercise path, the only way home requires one step at a time. Can Jesus usher them home quickly or in an instant? Absolutely! But often this is not the case. God grants people personal choice, and usually they take steps over time. Since some people spend decades walking away from God, we must often give them time and walk with them until they connect with Jesus in a life-changing way.

When I worked a part-time job pumping gas as a teenager, people stopped at the station for directions. Sometimes I gave people directions to their destinations. Other times, I could only send them closer to their goals. They'd need to stop and ask later for more directions. I didn't know how much I helped them, or if they ever reached their destinations. But I never worried about this. I did the best I could and let it go.

With evangelism, we're like gas attendants giving directions. People may go in and out of our lives. Some we know; others we don't. Our goal is to share what we know and give the best directions we can. Once we do our best, we can trust they get to their destinations. We can't literally accompany them. It's up to them to listen and seek more direction.

As we share, encourage, and help people, know that many people belong to the same team. We can add to that evangelistic team. As we grow in our ability to help others connect with Jesus, we can look for people hungry to win souls, for those who want their voices to be heard.

CHAPTER 20

A Weedlike Faith

One-generation Christianity ranks among the greatest enemies to the Great Commission. One-generation belief doesn't extend beyond an individual or a group of people, forgetting to multiply faith to those outside the individual, group, or into the next generation. This model often occurs in our churches. For example, a pastor leads a group of people to Jesus. As the pastor ages, so does the congregation. Eventually, both the pastor and congregation grow old and die. Someone fulfills the pastoral role, but often begins the process over again. In cases like this, the majority of church people participated in one generation of soul winning, often done by one person.

We appreciate the efforts of each pastor who evangelizes and builds a local church, and the people of that congregation, but God desires even more. Jesus lived the importance of training a group of soul winners, which we know as the Twelve Apostles. He also trained an additional seventy-two soul winners (Luke 10:1), and sent them out, along with many others. Whether He commissioned twelve or seventy-two, these followers continued His work of spreading the Gospel. Jesus then returned to heaven and sent the Holy Spirit so we could be empowered and also seek and save the lost throughout the whole earth.

Multi-Generational Ministry

I've chosen 2 Timothy 2:2 as my life scripture: "And the things you have heard me say in the presence of many witnesses entrust to reliable people who will also be qualified to teach others." I believe in this scripture so much, I named my non-profit ministry 4th Generation Ministries. This name represents spiritual multiplication beginning with Paul, a first-generation Christian, who taught Timothy. As generation two, Timothy passed on knowledge, wisdom, and spiritual impartation to reliable men, generation three. The third-generation believers taught others, generation four. This model for biblical growth and expansion can fulfill the Great Commission.

This model takes unrealistic pressure off any individual or ministry. Nobody can do it all. One of the world's best-known and beloved evangelists, Billy Graham, now embraces his sunset years. He's completed his major public ministry, preaching to more people and winning more souls in the twentieth century than anyone I know about. But at the end of his life, approximately five billion people don't know Jesus. [6] Is that his fault? No. He actively did his part. I'm just demonstrating that Jesus never meant the Great Commission to be a one-person show.

Jesus Chose Just a Few

Even Jesus didn't save everyone when He walked the earth. He is God and could have accomplished anything. But He chose to take on human limitations during His time on this planet. Actually, He said it was good for Him to leave so His followers could receive the Holy Spirit. He explained, "But very truly I tell you, it is for your good that I am going away. Unless I go away, the Advocate will not come to you; but if I go, I will send him to you" (John 16:7).

Jesus told His followers they would be filled with the Holy Spirit's power to do the Father's will. Because this power exists for all who truly follow Jesus—those filled with the Holy Spirit—we can help believers understand their calling and capability. We're to assimilate what we've learned and teach it to other reliable people. Let's not allow evangelism to stop with us! Let's not accept that most born-again, Bible-believing Christians in our generation live without winning one soul to Jesus.

As I said earlier, the best people to reach a community are the people who live in the community. We can spiritually multiply the generations in our churches and communities.

Strong, Weedlike Christianity

Weeds grow rapidly because they're native plants and perfectly suited for their location. Weeds thrive in their climate more than plants transplanted into a region. Plants brought in from someplace else may look nicer, but they require more time, energy, and resources. Weeds don't need special care. They're already suited for local conditions. They grow and multiply on their own.

We need weedlike Christianity. When we win people in our communities, they naturally thrive and multiply to reach others with the Gospel's life-transforming power. They know how to speak, relate, and connect in ways a pastor from the pulpit might not. No one person can connect with all of the community's cultures, races, education, or socio-economic levels to the degree multiple people in the community can.

This emphasizes why it's important to take the Gospel outside church walls so people meet face-to-face and house-to-house. God doesn't want His people to follow Him on just Sundays, but live by His saving faith every day. We need both the pastor and church people to reach the lost for Christ.

We live in a culture that's growing in its moral relativism, absence of faith, and many who are even anti-faith. The seminary-trained, intellectual pastor can be accurate with theology, but may not be received well in a community with less knowledge or a resistance toward spiritual or Biblical concepts. At the same time, someone with "just the spiritual basics" could share their authentic conversion experience quickly and clearly. These Christians already maintain connections with local people, and those friends, family, and coworkers witness the changes and growth in these believers' lives. That's when Christianity begins to spread like weeds.

Expressing the Gospel

Even though Christians with "just the basics" can powerfully share the Gospel, sometimes they still need and benefit from training to explain their changed lives. They personally admitted they're sinners, recognized their need for the Savior, and asked Jesus to forgive their sins. Through repentance, they changed the direction of their lives. Now they obediently follow Jesus and walk with Him each day. But much of this exists on an experiential level they can't put into words. These believers know what's happening, but without good teaching and discussion, can't clearly communicate their stories to others.

How do they explain, "I once was lost, but now am found?" How can they adequately put into words that the distance between them and God disappeared? How can they truly express, "I am forgiven?" When people can't find adequate words to describe their salvation and walk with God, they often express nothing.

When Christians share nothing, the Gospel stops moving forward. At this point, we can grab the opportunity build up and train these believers to put their salvation into words. We can begin with the people around us. Some might ask us for help. Or with the Lord's leading, we could ask people if they need help learning to share their faith.

Remember the Great Commission told us to make disciples, not just to evangelize the world. Discipleship begins with evangelism, but it doesn't end there. Once we win people to Jesus, we can help them establish relationships with Christians and a commitment to a church where they can grow and serve. We can also help them share their faith immediately. They don't need to know everything; just how to express what they know so far. Then we can encourage them toward a more complete understanding and memorization of scriptures to share with others.

When I begin to talk with people about sharing their personal faith story, I ask them to also learn how to teach others. People often learn best when they have to teach what they are learning to others. If I had a choice to preach to 100 people and share the Gospel, or sit down with ten people and teach them how to win souls, I'd talk to the smaller group. This would multiply soul winning. When people share the Gospel themselves, they add souls to God's Kingdom. When they train others to win souls, they multiply both soul winners and souls won!

The Power of Passion

If this involvement sounds like too much, don't forget we reach and teach with God's participation and power. Many times when I've preached to congregations or conferences, people approach me afterward and say it felt like I spoke directly to them. When I ask people what impacted them, each "heard" different principles. The Holy Spirit uses the words and shapes them to fit the listeners and minister to their specific needs. Likewise, in our one-on-one conversations, people will hear exactly what their souls need at that time. God uses broken vessels to speak words to another broken vessel, ministering to souls and spirits through those words.

Also remember that new believers can be some of the best evangelists in the world. They don't know a lot, but they understand God is real and He changes lives. This simple truth shared with passion and conviction often grabs people's attention. Some leaders focus on more mature Christians to evangelize, but at times it could be better to focus on those new in the Lord. The young in faith can actually be easier to train because of their passion and flexibility.

The blind man said he didn't know who healed him, but he knew "I was blind, but now I see" (John 9:25). That alone got people's attention. When people begin sharing their faith, passion can be more powerful than knowledge.

We can give people knowledge, but we can't instill passion. Passion bubbles up from within souls. Encourage people to share that passion. Help them express it in a biblically accurate way, but feed that passion! Passion changes lives. A passionate person with a little knowledge can outdo a person with just knowledge. Yes, a passionate well-trained person is the goal, but start with new believers. Take them on journeys to not only walk with Jesus, but to share Him with others. Teach them to let their voices be heard!

CHAPTER 21

Long-Term Passion and Suffering

Passion for winning souls can grow and change like a campfire or fireplace. To start a fire, we light paper with small sticks and get an initial burst of flame and heat. This is the exciting part of building a fire. It flares up. We get results for little effort. This type of fire can't last long, though, unless we keep throwing piles of small sticks on it. A steady flame is our eventual goal, so we place larger pieces of wood and logs beneath the paper and sticks. This part of the fire is more difficult to stoke, and it doesn't burn as bright. However, it burns much longer and gives off more heat in the long run.

Part of our Christian walk can resemble fire building. Our initial excitement and fire might not last as long as we'd like, and our passion to win souls changes from the frantic heat of new believers to the slow-and-steady burning of mature believers. The Kingdom of God needs both types. We need the almost wild, fired-up types and those slowly and steadily winning people to Jesus. Neither role is better than the other; we just fulfill different roles in the body of Christ.

We might also engage in seasons of evangelism, stepping away from slow-and-steady soul winning to a fired-up, passionate stage again. During these seasons of harvest, our voices sound louder and clearer, with decisions for Christ greater than other times. Whether clergy or laypeople, we all pass through different spiritual seasons.

When the Fire Burns Low

Even if we don't feel passionate about evangelism, God can still use us if we're willing. As I described earlier, one of my most effective soul-winning times occurred when I felt emotionally spent and not passionate about evangelism. During that season I regularly preached and hundreds of souls accepted the Lord, even though I'd lost my fire. It felt strange for God to use me even though I felt emotionally detached and burned out.

God can bring people to Christ through us "where we are" and that's heartening. But it's also unwise to stay in a slump. We can ask God to pull us out, and He will answer. Eventually, I cut back and dedicated myself to greater prayer and time with God. This refueled me, but God also accomplished some amazing things in spite of my spiritual condition. I'd tried to maintain an unsustainable pace and lifestyle, but He still used me as a broken and weak vessel to achieve His will. Be encouraged. God uses us despite our condition, but He also wants to build a fire in the belly to last over time.

Hunger versus Commitment

My spiritual dullness developed because I confused hunger with commitment. I reached more people than before, but in the busyness, I neglected my relationship with Jesus. I replaced spending time with Him with doing His work. I took for granted that God wanted to save people, and if I just focused on that, it would be enough to keep me going. My commitment to the Great Commission and to Jesus stayed full force, but my pursuit of God and passion for the lost slowly died. I thought my efforts and time commitment proved something. Because I put in the time, sweat, and energy, I considered that enough. All the while, my hunger for the lost slipped from me. I felt no less committed to Jesus, but my fire lost its heat. This eventually led to a lack of soul winning.

When I speak with people about their passion for winning souls, they often feel insulted. Like me, they confuse commitment to serving Jesus with a hunger to win souls. It's easy to do. Many commit to church and their personal relationship with Jesus, but never introduce anybody to Him. Or maybe they've reached sinners in the past, but Jesus doesn't focus on the "glory days." He emphasizes today.

Gladly, repentance can lead us back to the soul-winning fire. When someone lovingly told me I needed to repent, at first I got angry, but I listened. During these times I set aside more time for my Lord, sometimes starting with a bad attitude! But He wasn't afraid of my grumbling! As I spent time with God, He peeled away layers of pride, arrogance, and pain. He ministered to my heart, soul, and mind. One of my favorite scriptures says, "God opposes the proud, but gives grace to the humble" (James 4:6b, ESV). When we repent, it means telling God we don't know everything and can't do everything.

If we've grown dull and our passion to win souls lags, think about how long it took to reach that spiritual state. Christians gradually burn out or disconnect over time. If it took a slow process over several years, a weekend retreat won't fix it. God can touch us in a weekend, but often our minds and souls need time to fully recover. The longer it took to fade, the longer it could take to start that fire burning again.

Whatever the time period, our repentance demonstrates humility, which ushers in God's grace. Unfortunately, we often teach about grace in a narrow sense. We relegate it to the forgiveness of sins only. Salvation is the most significant and wonderful example of grace, but another definition also rings true. I learned it from my pastor, Dr. David Ireland. He says, "Grace is God's enabling power to do what He called you to do, and to be what He called you to be." Because we're created and called to win souls, when we repent, God's grace motivates us to evangelize.

Repentance also reveals God's presence like a beautiful sunrise. It's like walking outside in the early morning and feeling the sun on our faces. God smiles and stamps His approval on our soul-winning efforts. We can also expect Him to connect us with people who don't know Him. Yesterday is gone. Today is a new day.

Other Paths to Dullness

People who've grown up going to church can also have a dulled sense to soul winning. Knowing the Lord from an early age brings huge benefits as children develop under the Holy Spirit's guidance, the loving discipleship of godly parents, and a church's preaching and teaching. However, coming to Christ as children, these people didn't experience life-changing conversions. They simply fell in love with Jesus and grew up with that relationship.

With no Damascus Road experience, many lifetime church people, surrounded by Christians, don't develop a passion to win the lost. They can lack an understanding of those without Christ. Still, God can change hearts and lead these believers to unsaved people who need Him.

A passion for souls can also dampen from suffering. Even if we don't suffer for our faith, life serves us trials. People get sick. Financial problems overwhelm us. Miscarriages or infertility disappoint us. Problematic family and friends add up to pain. I don't want to sound trite or not compassionate, but many of the greatest men and women of God allowed suffering to fuel a fire to win souls. Paul wrote to the Thessalonians, "For we know, brothers loved by God, that he has chosen you, because our gospel came to you not simply with words, but also with power, with the Holy Spirit and with deep conviction. You know how we lived among you for your sake. You became imitators of us and of the Lord; in spite of severe suffering, you welcomed the message with the joy given by the Holy Spirit" (1 Thess. 1:4-6).

When I first read this scripture, I asked myself, *Have I really served God to the point of severe suffering? Have I really ever suffered?* I've had horrible experiences and stressful times, but I've never been persecuted or suffered solely for my faith. This is probably true for most Christians in America and Western countries.

While many of us will never physically suffer for our faith, we could face criticism, accusations, and judgments. If we don't want judgment or rejection, we might withdraw from God's call to win souls. Paul praised the Thessalonians because in spite of severe suffering, they gladly received and shared God's will for them. Does Christianity make us better? Absolutely! But is doesn't guarantee comfort.

One of the reasons for difficulty and suffering erupts from spiritual warfare. If we don't encounter resistance, we're not in the fight. Now some people can go overboard, claiming every bad experience and trial proves their holiness and commitment to God. This can be unbiblical and dysfunctional, but it does not negate the reality of spiritual warfare and resistance to God's purposes on earth.

Sometimes we need to ask, "What price am I willing to pay?"

The Apostle Paul worked harder than everyone during his time through many hardships (1 Cor. 15:10; 2 Cor. 4:6-10). He didn't just sit on a gift and calling. He worked, traveled, and suffered willingly to be fruitful in his labors. He got his hands dirty spiritually and physically, and the results grew the church. This apostle is our example. Despite everything, he let his voice be heard.

CHAPTER 22

In Our Lifetime

Dream with me for a minute. Wouldn't it be awesome if everyone on the planet heard the Good News of Jesus Christ, in a language and terms they understood, repetitively over time? Does that sound crazy?

Could we be crazy together and pursue this goal?

What more important goal could we spend our lives on?

Think about this. How much time and energy do we spend paying a mortgage? How many people actually pay it off before getting a new home? When my parents sold the house I grew up in, my father looked at me as he painted the foyer and said, "I was painting it when I moved in, and now I am painting it as I move out!" That was thirty-three years later. There must be more to life than buying a house, maintaining it for years, and selling it to move into the next one.

I think "the more important thing" is bringing people to Jesus for eternity.

We can't take a house with us when we die, but we can "take people to heaven" because we shared Christ with them.

If Everyone Took Part

What if we each spent just three hours a month purposely trying to win someone to Jesus? Let's do the math. If there are about one billion passionate Christ followers, at three hours per month for twelve months, that's 36 billion hours in the first year. How many souls could be added to heaven with this amount of soul-saving ministry?

Right now it is estimated there are about 2.5 billion "Christians" on planet Earth. About 1.5 billion are not actively engaged in sharing the gospel and are more cultural Christians than anything. There are approximately 1 billion, born-again, Bible-believing Christians here on our beloved planet Earth.[7] I have asked people at many churches, conferences, and major events if they are willing to spend the next twelve months winning just one person to Jesus. It is almost always unanimous that people would do this. If this happened, in year one, 1 billion would become 2 billion. If the same process continued, in year two, 2 billion Christ followers would become 4 billion. In year three, if it doubled again, 4 billion would become 8 billion.

The purpose of this example is not to say that we can win every person on the planet to Jesus in the next three years, but to demonstrate that when individuals embrace their personal responsibility to just win one soul to Jesus, that the cumulative effects can be extraordinary!

Either Staying or Sending

It's my prayer in the coming days we all begin or increase putting this book's principles to work. The Holy Spirit wants to fill and direct us with His power. He wants to change people's everyday lives and eternal destinies. Before the beginning of time, He ordained us to make disciples of all nations. Individually, we can't reach everyone, but we can reach someone.

We can't all "go" and become overseas missionaries, but we can win souls where we already live.

In fact, most Christians will never go where the Gospel is most needed in the world, or serve long-term in another country. Many places in the world are hostile or difficult to live in. For most Westerners, the cultural transition and differences are just too great, making the Gospel more difficult to share. Historically, sending Western missionaries into Third World countries winds up more expensive and less effective than raising up indigenous ministries.

Local people know the language, mindset, mannerisms, and culture in ways outsiders might never fully comprehend. Often indigenous people can live on less money and in conditions and circumstances outsiders find difficult or impossible. But that doesn't mean if we stay home, we don't get involved.

Most of us possess the ability to help finance a missionary or pastor in another country. For a dollar or two a day, a missionary in an impoverished country can serve in full-time ministry. Just a few dollars invested in a missionary can reap huge results over time. Many Christians think they don't have "extra" money, and the power to send the Gospel to the nations. But we do.

What we consider poor in America does not compare to the poverty in many countries. I worked with teens for over twenty years in many different settings and never met a student without clothing or food. I've worked with many considered low income, but I never had a student die of malnourishment or lack of medical care. Yet around the world, millions lack food, clothing, and medical aid. And many die daily without hearing the Gospel or meeting a Christian who lived Christ's love in front of them.

If we want our voices to be heard, we can give to missionaries and impoverished people. We can be heard around the world.

Some of my most rewarding donations have been to missionaries I'll never meet on this side of eternity. I look forward to meeting them in heaven and hearing how God used the few dollars I sent to India, Myanmar, and other countries. For a dollar a day, I sponsored a missionary who made my "sacrifice" trivial compared to what that person gladly endured for Christ. Someday in heaven I'll hear the stories of changed people, families, and villages I never visited. What an honor to give to that!

Ending Up in a Dump

Giving to missions is one of the best investments we can make. It produces eternal dividends. In contrast, what we own on earth will eventually end up in a garbage dump. Those $100 shoes? In the dump. That $40,000 car? In the dump. That $500,000 house could eventually host termites, water damage, and a sunken foundation. Bulldozed and in the dump! Every building ever erected will someday crumble. Every machine, boat, airplane, and electronic device will wear out, fall apart, break, rust, or get outdated. It will end up in a landfill and we'll move to the next investment that will also land in a dump. But souls in heaven will never decay; they will live forever in the presence of Almighty God!

There's no comparison as to what's most important.

Whether we drive a Chevy or Rolls Royce, remember both cars will pile up with others in a metal junkyard. If 100 souls could be saved by driving a less luxurious car, would it be worth it? It would be invaluable to the people, their families, and Jesus!

Imagine if every Christ follower not only shared the Gospel at home, but also sponsored a missionary someplace else. People love to give, but few donate to missionaries. I'm not mentioning or pushing certain mission organizations. I want everyone to embrace the concept, not an organization. I pray God births a passion in every Christian to sacrifice so others can live better on earth and eternally in heaven.

We can give to those willing to sacrifice for the call to save souls. These people live in hostile environments toward Christians. Pastors and missionaries in Muslim, Hindu, Communist, or other countries risk people or the government beating, imprisoning, persecuting, or killing them for sharing the Gospel. These mighty men and women of God live in obscurity, willing to lay down their lives for Christ. But they need us to support them financially. Our contribution would be small compared to theirs.

Can our spiritual fire within burn more intensely for them? We'll probably never lay down our lives, but we can support those who truly sacrifice. By sharing our resources, we can multiply voices sharing the Gospel at home and abroad.

See You in Eternity

God specializes in spiritual growth and multiplication. "Do the math" with Him. Don't live just paying a mortgage on earth. Build a mansion in heaven with plenty of rooms for the redeemed to visit. God wants to use each of us to win souls. Don't worry about too many details; focus on getting hungry to win souls. Become a humble student to Jesus, the great Master, and He'll teach you.

I pray just as Jesus left heaven to tread dirt roads and share the Gospel, Christians will leave their safety zones to walk streets, hallways, and neighborhoods, sharing the Good News with spiritually starving people. One day, our lives will end like a disappearing mist. Make life count by winning souls.

I look forward to meeting you in the days ahead—if not on this side of eternity, then in the next. And I can't wait to meet many souls in heaven because you let your voice be heard!

Notes

Introduction

Page 03 – [1] Kennedy, D. James. Evangelism Explosion. Wheaton, IL: Tyndale House Publishers, 1970. p. 6

Page 03 – [2] Center for the Study of Global Christianity, "Christianity in its Global Context, 1970–2020: Society, Religion, and Mission," *Christianity in Its Global Context*, June 2013, http://www.gordonconwell.edu/resources/documents/1ChristianityinitsGlobalContext.pdf.

Chapter 04: Giving God Away

Page 31 – [3] Robert Frost, Mountain Interval (New York: Henry Holt and Company, 1920); Bartleby.com, 1999, www.bartleby.com/119/.

Chapter 13: Give Somebody a Reason

Page 89 – [4] Goodreads.com, http://www.goodreads.com/quotes/22155-i-like-your-christ-i-do-not-like-your-christians.

Chapter 17: Defeating the Enemy Called Fear

Page 119 – [5] Mark Twain, *Puddi'nhead Wilson* (Avon, Conn.: Heritage Press, 1974).

Chapter 20: A Weedlike Faith

Page 146 – [6] http://www.pewforum.org/2011/12/19/global-christianity-exec/?beta=true&utm_expid=53098246-2.Lly4CFSVQG2lphsg-KopIg.1.

Chapter 22: In Our Lifetime

Page 160 – [7] http://www.worldometers.info/world-population/.

Previous Books Written

Infusion: Receive. Grow. Give it Away…

Wounded Heart: Keys to Overcoming Life's Pain and Disappointments

People Matter to God: Experiencing Personal Transformation and Sharing it With Others

Transformation: The 7 Pillars of a Legacy Minded Man

Co-authored with Joe Pellegrino
www.legacymindedmen.com

God Belongs in My City

Co-authored with Daniel Sanabria
www.Godbelongsinmycity.com

To Connect with Jack Redmond, please go to:

www.jackredmond.org

www.ingramcontent.com/pod-product-compliance
Lightning Source LLC
Jackson TN
JSHW020708190426
101040JS00034B/299

* 9 7 8 1 6 3 0 4 7 6 9 6 0 *